How to Get Your Competition Fired

(without Saying Anything Bad about Them)

How to Get Your Competition Fired

(without Saying Anything Bad about Them)

Using The Wedge® to Increase Your Sales

Randy Schwantz

WILEY

John Wiley & Sons, Inc.

Published by John Wiley & Sons, Inc., Hoboken, New Jersey.
Published simultaneously in Canada.

The Wedge®, The Wedge® logo, and Selling Is a Contact Sport® are registered trademarks of Schwantz and Associates, Inc.

For general information on our other products and services please contact our Customer Care Department within the United States at (800) 762-2974, outside the United States at (317) 572-3993 or fax (317) 572-4002.

Wiley also publishes its books in a variety of electronic formats. Some content that appears in print may not be available in electronic books. For more information about Wiley products, visit our web site at www.Wiley.com.

Library of Congress Cataloging-in-Publication Data:
Schwantz, Randy.
    How to get your competition fired (without saying anything bad about them) : using The Wedge to increase your sales / Randy Schwantz.
        p.   cm.
    ISBN 0-471-70311-7 (cloth)
    1. Selling.   2. Sales management.   3. Competition.   I. Title.
    HF5438.25.S3392   2005
    658.85—dc22
2004017334

Printed in the United States of America.

10   9   8

*To Lori, one of the world's greatest jugglers,
a champion of kids, horses, and basketball, my pillar,
the apple of my eye, my one and only.*

I also want to dedicate this book to you, the salesperson. The work you do in keeping the wheels of commerce turning is indispensable. My fondest wish is that this book will help you achieve your own goals sooner and provide excellent, proactive service to more clients.

Contents

Preface   *ix*

Introduction   The #1 Obstacle to Most
              New Business   1

PART I   The Strategy to Win   **17**

  1 The Wedge   19

  2 Finding Your Winning Difference   41

PART II   The Tactics That Work   **65**

  3 The Wedge Sales Call   67

  4 Discovering the Pain—The Problem Phase   79

  5 Proposing a Remedy—The Solution Phase   107

  6 Getting Your Competition Fired—
        The Commitment Phase   121

PART III   Changing the Way Selling Is Done   **133**

  7 Individual Success   135

  8 The Wedge Sales Culture   147

CONTENTS

9   For Buyers Only   183

10   For Current Providers Only   189

11   The Wedge Flight Plan: A Quick Review   193

References   201

Index   203

About the Author   209

Preface

I have more than 200 books on my bookshelf about selling. They all say pretty much the same thing, that selling involves two people—the seller and the buyer. They say if the seller can build a relationship with the buyer, find out what the buyer needs, then bring in what the buyer needs, the seller will be rewarded.

The reality is that there are three people in the selling interview—the buyer, the seller, and the unseen current provider. Not only do you have to be great at building relationships, you'd better be great at busting the incumbent relationship.

The biggest challenge with traditional selling methods is that they don't have a strategy for dealing with the third party, the incumbent. Unless you have a strategy for driving a wedge between the buyer and the current provider in order to get your competition fired, the chance is very good that the incumbent will leverage the existing relationship with the client (your prospect) to get a "last look" and match your proposal. You've just been rolled.

So the question is, how do you *Get Your Competition Fired* without saying anything bad about them? Read on. . . .

The #1 Obstacle to Most New Business

This book is the result of more than 10,000 hours I have spent working with salespeople.

A lot of them, perhaps like you, were very motivated, smart, hardworking, and yet frustrated. They were frustrated because they were not achieving the high goals they had set for themselves. For them, hard work did not always mean a higher income.

These were people who appeared to be doing everything right. They were excellent communicators and great relationship builders. They listened to their prospects. They were helpful and friendly. They brought back great proposals at great prices. And on too many occasions, they still did not get the business.

What I learned from my experience has helped many of these people achieve their personal goals of doubling or tripling their incomes, having more time for their families and other personal relationships, and realizing the professional success that had escaped them for so long.

How did they do it? Did they work longer hours? Did they call on more prospects? No. In fact, they quit playing the numbers game. Instead, they focused their limited time and energy on overcoming the number one obstacle to selling most new business—their competition.

The Garden-Variety Sales Call

Many salespeople, when they target a prospect, are naturally eager to call on the prospect and start building a relationship. After doing a limited amount of research, they contact the prospect and schedule an initial appointment. The typical sales call follows a predictable pattern, going through three stages.

Stage 1

In the first stage, the salesperson has learned enough to ask questions that make sense. He or she has done some research (not a lot yet), and is set on creating a friendly rapport to get things off to a good start. The conversation goes something like this:

> *Seller:* "Hello, Ray. I really appreciate your seeing me today. How are things going?"
>
> *Prospect:* "Pretty good, Bill. How about you?"
>
> *Seller:* "Oh, fine. Thanks for asking. Tell me, how's business?"
>
> *Prospect:* "Everything is going fine."
>
> *Seller:* "Well, as you know, I'm with Greater Smithville Community Bank. We've been in business since 1953, and we've got 12 branches now in the Smithville metropolitan area, not including our other ATM locations. We're proud to be the banker for three other local firms in your industry. We sure would like to have a chance to handle your banking needs for you. Whom do you bank with now?"
>
> *Prospect:* "We've been with Giant National Bank for six years, ever since they bought Smithville First, our previous banker."

Seller: "How's it going with Giant National?"

Prospect: "Fine."

Seller: "Any problems with service?"

Prospect: "Not really anything to speak of."

Seller: "What are your gross annual sales, Ray, more or less?"

Prospect: "Well, last year they were $30 million, and this year I think we'll be at about $42 million."

Seller: "I see. Any concerns with the rates Giant National gives you on loans, certificates of deposit, other financial products?"

Prospect: "No. They've done a good job. Their rates seem to be about normal."

Seller: "What about your line of credit? Have they treated you right on that?"

Prospect: "Well, it could always be a little more, I suppose."

Seller: "What about fees and other extra charges?"

Prospect: "Nothing special. They ding us on something occasionally, but for the most part they're pretty normal."

Seller: "Great. Ray, I'd like to put together a proposal for you. I'd like to lay out what we can do for you as your banker as you continue to grow. If we can improve your line of credit and potentially save you some money on other things, is there any reason why we can't do business?"

Prospect: "No, not at all. We'd be happy to entertain what you've got."

Bill takes the information back to the main office, and brings up the "Proposal" form on his computer screen. He starts adapting it to fit the size of Ray's company, and he drops the name of Ray's company into the boilerplate language. He consults the Giant National marketing materials he has on file, looking up Giant National's typical rates and charges for small business customers like Ray. When his vice president for business development, Ruth, asks him how the new business appointment went, he tells her that the prospect does not have any real problems to speak of, but would be interested in an expanded line of credit, which Greater Smithville Community Bank can do, and in saving some on fees and other charges. They nod their heads in agreement.

Stage 2

After Bill has completed his proposal, he puts it together in a slick packaged presentation, and he calls Ray and sets up an appointment.

> *Seller:* "Thanks for having me back out, Ray. I think you'll like what I'm going to tell you."
>
> *Prospect:* "Sounds good. What have you got?"
>
> *Seller:* "Well, basically we can expand your line of credit by another $300,000, plus we can waive or reduce a lot of the annoying charges you pay for things like online bill payment, loan application fees, and detailed summary statements. In fact, we'll even reimburse the ATM fees you pay when you withdraw money from your business account

while you're traveling anywhere in the United States. So what do you think?"

Prospect: "Well, Bill. It looks pretty good. I appreciate what you came up with. We'll definitely consider your proposal. Let me look over what you put together, and we can talk next week."

Seller: "Well, Ray, this is a pretty competitive proposal. Any reason we can't get started now?"

Prospect: "Bill, I like what you've got here. I would just like a few days to study it some. Please call me in a few days."

Seller: "That's fine, Ray. I'll check back with you in a few days."

Bill returns to his office and he runs into Ruth again. When she asks him how it went, he tells her, "Terrific. I'd say we've got an excellent chance. I've got a nice rapport going with Ray. He likes what we brought to the table. I expect we'll hear something in the next few days."

Stage 3

Meanwhile, Ray calls his banker at Giant National to talk about the upcoming year. He asks what Giant National might be able to offer based on his growth, and whether he might be able to save any on his fees and charges. The banker gets the feeling that something is going on, and he asks Ray if he has some concerns. Ray tells him that, yes, he is considering making a change, but he wanted to see what Giant National could do before he did. At that point,

Ray's banker asks for a visit, and he gets in his car to go to see Ray.

Current Banker: "Ray, I appreciate your call today. I wanted to tell you how much your business means to us. As you know, we've always been willing to jump through hoops to meet your financial needs. I don't know who you're talking to, or what they might be telling you, but I'm sure we can expand your line of credit and be as competitive on fees and charges as anyone. If we can do that, do you see any reason why we can't continue our relationship? I know we can work out whatever might be bothering you."

Bill's Prospect: "You've done a good job for us. If you can help me out on the things I've mentioned, we'll stay with you."

Current Banker: "I'm sure we can, Ray."

A few days later, Bill calls Ray. He reaches Ray's voice mail, and leaves a message that he is checking in. The next day, Ray finally returns his call.

Seller: "Hi, Ray. So how did we do?"

Prospect: "You were really thorough, and I want to thank you for going through the trouble of getting us the proposal. I guess what it came down to is that the line of credit issue and the fees and charges weren't something we couldn't deal with without changing horses right now."

Seller: "Okay, Ray. I hear you. Let me do this. I'll keep in touch, and maybe I can come back out there later this year and see where you are then."

Bill makes a note to call on Ray again in six months. When Ruth sticks her head in the door to see how it went, Bill explains, "Maybe we couldn't improve Ray's situation enough compared with what Giant National is doing for him. But, anyway, he seems too satisfied right now to switch banks. I'll keep after it, though."

Bill just got "rolled." It happens to many salespeople who go in slinging their sales pitch and often are too ready to offer a quote to try to save the prospect money. The real problem is that Bill had a weak sales strategy. Although he made an effort to find out about any problems or frustrations that his prospect might be having with Giant National Bank, his process did not find any that made a big enough difference. Nor did he take into account that Giant National already had the relationship, and probably would get—and did get—a chance to explain its own advantages, improve Ray's line of credit, and lower or waive a fee here and there when he called to compare. Bill also failed to differentiate Greater Smithville Community Bank from Giant National. He merely talked about the fact that his bank had a local presence, its years in business, its locations, its customers—the things that make most banks the same.

In short, Bill made no effort to identify any truly meaningful differences between his own bank and his competition, Giant National. He identified nothing that would strongly motivate Ray to consider switching. As a result, he never really had anything to sell other than a price difference and the same willingness to expand his prospect's line of credit that other banks have. Like many salespeople who rely on traditional selling methods, he got rolled.

Tactics You Can Use Right Away

In this book I show how to overcome the natural advantage of the current provider, and how to gain an edge over any competitor. I give you proven tactics that you can use to get your competition fired from an account, or from being considered for an open account that you want, without your having to say anything bad about your rivals. Together, these tactics and the strategy on which they are based are known as The Wedge.

If you are like me, you have sat through many sales courses and read the standard books. I remember walking into many of these classes saying to myself, "If I can get just one good idea, this is probably worthwhile." Many of the good ideas that I got, though, were so conceptual that it took a lot of time to convert them into day-to-day, practical methods that would help me sell more now and make more money. It was like going to a supermarket for dinner rather than going to a restaurant. At a supermarket, you have to buy all the ingredients, take them home, and prepare your meal yourself rather than walking in, ordering something off the menu, and leaving 30 minutes later satisfied.

Unlike traditional selling, The Wedge is a ready-to-eat meal. This book gives you simple, practical techniques that have worked for others. I am not talking about ideas, concepts, and theories that leave it up to you to figure out how to apply them. I am talking about no-nonsense, easy-to-grasp tactics that you can start using tomorrow morning to get results.

The Wedge is not an alternative to Selling 101. As we discuss The Wedge, I assume that you know many of the basics of selling—how to create rapport, effective communications skills, and so on. Unavoidably, some of the ground we cover may sound familiar to you. However, you will notice an important difference. The Wedge, with its focus on the relationship between your prospect and your competitor, takes the selling process to a higher level. It is more like Sales 401, building on what you already know.

The Wedge is based on a practical reality that traditional selling largely ignores. Conventional wisdom says a selling situation involves two parties—a seller and a buyer. Conventional wisdom is wrong. Most major selling opportunities involve three parties—you, the prospect, and your competition. Until you have a strategy for dealing with your opponents, you do not have a sure prospect.

The salesperson who currently has an account is particularly in the driver's seat. He or she already has the relationship with the prospect, and is going to do everything possible to keep the business. Therefore, to create an opportunity to win the account, you must first drive a wedge between your prospect and the provider. Of course, here is the problem. You cannot walk into prospects' offices and start bad-mouthing the companies whose services they made the decision to employ. Do that, and you might as well say, "Let me get this straight, Joe. Were you the person who actually hired these people?"

Your challenge is—without criticizing your competition—to help your prospects see that they are being underserved by your rivals leading them to decide on their own that they would be better off if they switched or gave their business to you. Learn how to do that, and you can start winning larger, more profitable accounts faster than you ever have.

Facing a Fundamental Truth

I also wrote this book because other sales books (and I have read most of them) do not address a fundamental truth about selling. Most of the time, someone must lose for you to win. That is the truth.

Yet, calculating how to get people fired is often considered harsh at best and unethical at worst. Civilized people do not set out to take bread off the tables of their competitors. So we fancy selling as a solo sport, like figure skating. You skate out onto the ice. You smile and do your routine, hoping that your artistry and technical skills will impress the judges enough for you to win the gold. You nail your triple axels, and become one with the music. When you have finished your presentation, you take a bow and wait for the judges to hold up their cards. You wait confidently, thinking to yourself, "I know I'm going to get a 10." Blissful and expectant, you look at the crowd on the edge of its seats, sharing this moment with you, and then . . .

11

Wham!

Just like in hockey, someone comes skating out of nowhere, knocks you off your imagined pedestal, and skates away with your medal. Welcome to the real world, where selling is a contact sport, where often the prospect and a person who already has the business are the home team, and where you are the visiting underdog.

The Golden Rule

Even when they realize that selling is a contact sport, some salespeople feel squeamish about waking up each day and figuring out whose accounts they can take away. Somehow, we have gotten the idea that getting people fired replaces the Golden Rule with the cynical notion that gold rules, and decency be damned. "Hi, honey. I'm home. Guess what? I got three people axed today. Pretty cool, huh?"

This notion is 180 degrees wrong. If you are not successful at getting buyers out of inferior relationships and into better ones, you are leaving those buyers stuck with mediocre service for weeks, months, or years. If you do not help them see the difference and gain the courage to fire— or not to hire—your competition, then you are letting them down. You are doing unto them what you would not want them to do unto you. This is especially important today, when every company must measure up to a general standard in order to stay in business and do well.

If your company cannot do a better job than your rival, then yes, it would be wrong for you to bust the relationship only to then give your new client inferior service;

but if you are truly better, then you owe it to yourself and your prospect to do all you can to get your competition fired so that you can take over the account.

The Virtue of Being Fired

For the intelligent salesperson, getting fired for the right reason is a blessing in disguise. For average salespeople, it is just something bad that happened to them. Smart salespeople, however, use the experience to focus on what they were doing wrong, and how they can become better. To the degree that the threat of losing an account makes them work harder to win and keep their customers, that is a good outcome, too. In either case, seeking to have them fired sorts the deck of business relationships into pairs that are healthier and more productive all the way around.

Getting unworthy service providers fired is also good for the economy. When you lose a sale because you did not have a strategy for taking out your competitor, it is not just a setback for you. Everybody loses. You lose time. Your company loses money. Your prospect loses the benefit of what you failed to sell. And all of us pay higher prices for the goods and services we buy as your company passes along its higher-than-necessary "sales acquisition costs."

Why The Wedge Works

If you are like me, you are skeptical about theories and abstract models when it comes to selling. You know how things work in the real world. No course or textbook can fully capture what a salesperson goes through. The Wedge is not merely a model. It is a complete selling system with a proven set of tactics wrought from actual sales experience. It is a step-by-step process; you and your company can use it to drill down and find your true competitive advantage, break it down into simple chunks, and put these chunks into questions to ask your prospects. These questions will get them to see that they are being underserved and that they would be better off with you—without your having said saying anything bad about your competition or telling your prospects how great you are.

Your Real Competitive Advantage

The Wedge works also because it is based on finding and using your real competitive advantage. What do I mean by real competitive advantage?

Your company and others basically compete on three things: price, product, and service. When it comes to price, your competitors in most cases can beat your price if they choose to. How great a salesperson does it take to sell on price? Moreover, price differences among comparable services and products are usually too marginal to be decisive. There is no sustainable competitive advantage in price.

As far as most products are concerned, there is not a lot of real differentiation among them within the same category. If you do offer a product with a truly meaningful difference, then you can leverage that. More often than not, however, product differences are not major enough to make a significant difference in the salability of those products. So there is no sustainable competitive advantage here, either.

When it comes to service, companies provide reactive and proactive service. Reactive service is the way you respond to client problems, concerns, and issues that arise. Do you have good people who promptly return phone calls? Do you effectively troubleshoot situations brought to your attention by your clients? Most companies do a reasonably good job of reactive service. Therefore, reactive service seldom gives a business a powerful competitive edge.

Of all of these competitive areas, proactive service offers the greatest potential for you to differentiate yourself from the competition and win new business. Here is a mantra to repeat: *"My job as a salesperson is to proactively control the experiences of my clients, making their future more predictable."* You need to give your prospects and your clients a defined process where things do not fall through the cracks. That is what you have to sell. This book discusses in detail what proactive service means. Essentially, proactive service is the day-to-day things you do to control the experiences of your clients and make their future more predictable.

Remember Bill, the banker? He offered no proactive service to make his prospect's future more predictable, such as a regular business plan review. He tried to sell on price, and he got rolled by the prospect's current bank, which merely had to react to his offer to leverage its incumbent position and keep the account.

Proactive service is your number one responsibility,

and the surest way to win and keep new accounts. Most companies do not take advantage of this reality. If they focus on service, they focus on reactive service. They do not clearly articulate the specific things they do proactively that make them different and better. That is your competitive advantage, and you can leverage that competitive advantage using The Wedge.

Most prospects are being underserved in some way. Many of them are in business relationships that, for various reasons, they lack the incentive to change. Some of them are in the market looking for what you offer, but they have a provider in place that has always been able to persuade them not to switch. Others are shopping anew, but have low service expectations that give your inferior competitors an opening. If you could get these underserved businesses to realize for themselves that they would be better off buying from you, that could be worthwhile, couldn't it?

THE STRATEGY
TO WIN

The Wedge

Selling is like flying. If you do not land safely, nothing else matters. And so it is with sales. It is about setting your wheels on the runway safely and getting paid. If you do not win the deal, what is the point? Few salespeople get paid to prospect and present. What they get paid for is to win. No, I am not saying your life is at stake. But if you are going to invest your time in seeing a prospect, why not at least have a strategy to maximize your chance of winning the business?

As I spent my first 5,000 hours coaching and listening to salespeople, I kept asking myself: What is it that makes them crash? What prevents them from landing safely and getting paid?

One problem is that, in most cases, someone already has the account. As you come in for a landing seeking to touch down on the runway and close the deal, your competition—the incumbent provider who already has the account—is waiting in the bushes beside the tarmac with a bazooka, ready to protect the relationship that he or she has with your prospect. His or her goal is to knock you out of the sky before you can land, by interceding to get "last look," matching your price, and keeping the business. In sales, it's called getting rolled.

The second biggest problem is that you do not differentiate yourself enough to be seen by your prospect as better than your competition. Your ability to gain altitude is in direct proportion to your differentiation. The higher you fly, the safer you are. When you lack clear differentiation, you are flying around at 100 feet avoiding water towers and small hills. You never gain the altitude you need, and you come crashing down.

These two problems—the competition's relationship with your prospect and a lack of clear differentiation by you, the seller—are what cause you to crash.

Stop Selling and Start Winning

Many sellers have made an art out of telling their stories, putting together slick presentations, and finding numerous other ways to impress their clients. All too often, the emphasis and spotlight are on themselves. They are masters at selling.

Winning is about understanding that there are *three* people in most selling situations—you, the prospect, and the competition, not just you and the prospect. Your job is to win by using your differentiation to get your prospects to discover for themselves that they are being underserved by their current providers, without saying anything bad about those providers. Your task is to get them to see that what they need, and want to buy, is what you have, without your having to sell them on it.

Many salespeople work hard at getting appointments, going on their sales calls, and hoping that the calls turn into wins. See enough people, and the law of averages will take care of you. A predictable percentage of the people you meet with will buy.

It is the mentality of a slot machine player. If you pull the lever over and over, you can count on winning enough to keep reinvesting your quarters at least for a while. The problem is that playing the numbers game in selling is like playing the numbers game in gambling. In the long run, you will probably wind up with a pocketful of nothing even though you hit a small jackpot on occasion. Psychologists call this "random positive reinforcement." In sales, it is a prescription for average earnings or worse. If you have any desire to take your income to the next level, you are going to need a new strategy—one that is not based on the luck of the draw, the numbers game, or hope. You need a strategy that will enable you to stop selling and to start winning.

A Brief History of Selling

Back in the agrarian days when professional salespeople went from town to town peddling their goods from horse-drawn wagons, nobody much thought of selling as a science. Then came the industrial revolution. Factories sprang up. Railroads linked markets. The stakes got higher. In response, factory owners started to organize teams of selling agents to pitch their mass-produced wares. Selling became a more serious occupation. With a company's workforce counting on sales to feed its families, the salesperson was relied on as the go-to individual to keep those McCormick reapers and Gillette razor blades moving. If salespeople did not get the job done, they could screw up a lot more lives than just their own.

By the early twentieth century, salespeople were firmly established as the engine driving the wheels of commerce. Around the same time, thanks to Sigmund Freud, Carl Jung, and others, psychology was catching on as a window into the workings of the human mind. In light of this, it occurred to more than a few business leaders, "Hmmm. Maybe there's a way we can improve the selling process itself."

First came feature benefit selling. Start with the seller, and make the seller a better pitch deliverer for the service or product. The focus was on improving the seller's communications skills, using what psychology was finding out about how buyers think. Cite the feature, and mention the benefit. In other words: Here is what it is. Here is what it does. Here is how it is good for you. And then go to a trial close, testing your prospect's inclination to buy.

The creation of a supersalesperson who could sell anyone anything proved to be an illusive goal. Besides, even if it were possible for sales scientists to teach someone how to sell screen doors to submarine manufacturers, the sales profession in that case would lose its ultimate source of survival—customer satisfaction. To deal with this dilemma, the sales gurus developed what became known as consultative selling. Start with the buyer, and figure out how you can satisfy the buyer's needs. The focus was on helping buyers get what they want. A skilled consultative seller became one with the buyer. He or she was the buyer's advocate and partner. He or she helped the buyer make the right decision. Whereas feature benefit selling was about trying to convince the buyer overtly and directly, consultative selling was about creating a cozier relationship with the buyer and leveraging that relationship.

Consultative selling remains the rage today. It is an

excellent way to sell—except when it doesn't work. Too often consultative selling does not work, even when it should. Why? The problem is that it is based on an incomplete model of two parties, the buyer and the seller. In reality, there is often a third party, the incumbent provider. In most cases, current providers will get last look. They will leverage their existing relationship to get back in with your prospect—their client—and tell your prospect that they can match your price, your service, and your product. They will steal your ideas and your hard work, and more often than not keep the business. When this happens, you have been rolled. You crashed.

If you are selling in an industry where the current provider is not really an issue, where the buyer is not buying products regularly or being serviced on a consistent basis, this may not be as relevant to you. You may be getting by on feature benefit selling, or you may get satisfactory results using the consultative approach; but if you are in a business where somebody has to lose for you to win, then you know what I am talking about. You need to take out the current provider in order to get paid. If you can't take out the incumbent, then you don't put groceries on the table tonight, no one is going to buy diapers for the baby, and there won't be a summer cottage. If you do not have a definitive strategy for driving a wedge between your prospect and the person who already has the business, you probably do not have a real prospect.

To win in the real world where there are sellers, buyers, and current providers, you must not only be good at building relationships; you must also be good at breaking relationships apart. You need to know how to get your competition fired. In situations where you are competing for an open account against other salespeople, you face the same kind of challenge. For you to win, your competitors must lose. In other words, you must get your competition fired from consideration.

Is Your Focus on Selling or Winning?

In 1896, the Italian economist Vilfredo Pareto came up with what is known today as the 80/20 Rule. Pareto showed that, in any given population, about 20 percent of the people will tend to end up with about 80 percent of the wealth. This is why, for a typical sales force, the 20 percent who are go-getters will tend to bring in 80 percent of the revenue. Pareto was onto something; and now we know how this imbalance of earnings happens in the sales profession. It is because there are two kinds of salespeople: those who seek just another chance to present, and those who go into every sales call with a strategy to win.

Let me ask you a question. What is the most important part of a car? Is it the engine? The brakes? The key? The driver? It is really none of these. The most important part of a car is the missing part. Without that part, the car will go nowhere, or at least nowhere safely. So what is the most important part of selling? It, too, is the missing part; and, in most cases, the missing part is having a strategy to get your competition fired.

Presenting features and benefits to a prospect is helpful, but not enough. Being consultative is worthy and honorable, but often is also not enough. Perhaps it has never happened to you, where you listened to your prospect carefully, you developed a proposal based on his or her needs, and then you presented it to your prospect effectively. It solved the problems your prospect had and the pricing was competitive, but then you found out the incumbent rep had kept the business. Banging your head against the wall, you asked yourself, "What happened?" You know what happened. The incumbent rolled you. He or she matched your proposal, and the incumbent won and you lost. Yes, you need to build relationships. But you already know that, and you do it. What many salespeople don't do is look at the relationship between the prospect and their competition. That is the missing part. There is no highly effective strategy (other than The Wedge) for getting your prospect to see the incumbent in a negative way. That is one reason that 80 percent of salespeople bring in only 20 percent of the revenue.

Before you put this book back on the shelf, concerned that The Wedge is a negative force, an immoral way of selling, let me ask you this: Do you own a home? Is it insured? Is there any chance that in the past few years you bought something new of great value? Here's why I ask. When your personal insurance agent came to your home 30 days before your most recent renewal to do an exposure analysis, and your agent got out a form listing all the potential areas where you could have a loss, and your agent told you what was currently covered and not covered in case of a loss, so that you wouldn't have to worry about having a claim that you would have to pay out of your own pocket, were you comfortable with how your agent went through that process? Unless you have an absolutely remarkable insurance agent, there is a pretty good chance that you haven't seen your agent in years, maybe never. Perhaps you don't care that it's been that way. Maybe you're so well-to-do that, if you had something stolen or if your house were destroyed by a fire or tornado, you wouldn't care whether your insurance company replaced it for you.

Let me take this one step further and ask you this: How many times have you received a call at home in the evening from someone wanting to give you a quote on homeowner's insurance? How did you respond? You probably said, "No. I'm happy." Doesn't it make sense to you now? If you had a way to get your prospects to see how they are being underserved by their incumbent sales representatives without your saying anything bad about those reps, while getting your prospects to see how great you are without having to tell them, wouldn't that shorten the amount of time it takes to win new business?

In short, what is missing from traditional selling methods is an emphasis on getting your competition fired without saying anything bad about them.

Reality Check

Let us assume that you are ready to go in there with a strategy to win. You are going to help your prospects see what they cannot get from your competitor that they could be getting from you. You are going to leverage that to create a wedge between your prospects and your competitors that you can use to get these accounts. In a perfect world, this would work every time. Unfortunately, that is not the world in which you and I live.

As a salesperson, you likely have a pretty good client retention rate. How many times have your clients shopped around and then said to you, "Can you do this?" In one industry I have worked with, the commercial property and casualty insurance industry, agents enjoy a whopping 92 percent retention rate among their current clients. Is it because they are God's gift to insurance? No. It is because they have the relationship with the client, and they can get last look. How many times have you leveraged your relationships with your clients to get last look? You probably do it all the time.

In football, if you are the quarterback, you know that one way to get five free yards is to bark out signals and get the defense to jump offside. If you are on defense, you do just the opposite. You move out of your three-point stance, doing your best to get the offensive linemen to move prematurely, and if one does, then you get five free yards.

When you are the incumbent and your goal is to retain your account, you operate under a different set of rules from the rules you would use if you were a seller trying to get a new account. For example, have you been to Louisiana? If you have, you know that everyone there likes to hunt and fish. How do you create relationships there? You just take your buddy hunting. After a couple of cold beers or a little jack on the rocks, you can forge a pretty good relationship. Why is this important? It's pretty obvious. When someone comes after your account, you just remind your client of the good times on the hunting lease.

You tell your buddy that if he'd just give you a chance, you are sure that you could make some adjustments in your price as well as tweak the service a bit. When all is said and done, who's going to keep the business?

So, there are certain rules of the game that you can use to keep your advantage with your client. Now, turn the tables. When you are talking to a new prospect, is the current provider not trying to do the same thing to you? This is the reality of selling that you have to deal with every day. You cannot be in denial about it. You cannot be naive. To win, you have to acknowledge it exists, and do something about it—and as you do, there are two other realities you will be confronting.

Why Prospects Lie

Early in my career as a sales coach and consultant, I was a little naive and, at one point, I was working for three different Dallas insurance agencies. I spent some time talking with one of the agencies about how to win a particular prospect. Later, when I was talking to the second of the three agencies, it turned out that it was trying to win the same prospect. The third agency I was working for, you guessed it, had the prospect as a client.

About a month after coaching the two agencies pursuing the prospect, I learned that the incumbent agency had kept the account. So I went to talk to a guy I knew at the first agency, and I asked him what had happened. "Man, we got killed on price," he told me. Then I went to the second agency, asked the same question, and they told me the same thing. They, too, said they got killed on price.

So I went to see a friend who worked for the incumbent agency, mentioning to him that I had heard his agency kept the account and that the other two agencies lost out on price. "Who told you that?" he asked. "Want to hear the real story?"

"Sure," I replied. "What happened?"

He then told me that his two rivals' quotes had actually been lower than those of his agency. He said that he had had to take his underwriter to lunch (and buy two bottles of wine) in order to persuade him to lower the price so his client would stay with him. I walked out of our meeting thinking, "It's pretty amazing what a prospect will tell the loser to get off the hook of feeling bad."

The more I thought about it, the more I understood the full significance. It was one of those "aha" moments that made me start asking a lot of questions to get to the heart of how selling is actually done. Prospects do lie to salespeople, and this is one more example of the power of the incumbent who already has the prospect's business. Prospects tell white lies in part because they are tight with their incumbents and have no serious intention of switching. It is not that they are bad people. It is human nature. By pretending to be interested seriously in your offering, they can get a free education. If you are willing to sit down with them and enlighten them about what you offer, why would they not want to take advantage of your generosity? They can use you to find out what is going on in the market. You are a free source of useful knowledge to help their companies, a source of innovative ideas and current best thinking. Your prospects are probably nice people, too. They do not want to hurt your feelings, so they give you the chance to present, to try to sell them. They might even let you buy them lunch. They want you to think good things about their companies. When you have finished presenting, they will shake your hand, promise to stay in touch, wish you well, and toss your business card into the wastebasket as you exit the front door.

Losing with the Perfect Proposal

Sometimes, though, you hit it off with a prospect immediately. Something clicks, you instantly connect, and the prospect asks you to put a deal together. You come back with exactly the solution you were asked for. The service is right. The price is right. The chemistry is good. Everything looks perfect. Have you won the account? Not yet. Why? Because nobody has dealt with the person who already has the account. You cannot expect your prospect to take care of this for you. He or she does not want to call up Phil and say, "Hi, Phil. I just called to let you know it's over. Other than that, have a great day."

In the real world, Phil is going to find out about your proposal. Unless your prospect learned that morning that Phil had been selling inside information about the prospect's company to its rivals, he or she is going to confide in Phil that your proposal is being seriously looked at. That is a signal to Phil to counter. So he will spring into action, taking advantage of his position as the incumbent provider. He will get last look, match your offer, and keep the business. He will do whatever it takes to keep your prospect happy. He will relieve your prospect of the unpleasant notion that he or she has to fire someone to get the desired result.

Never underestimate the power of the current provider. He or she has the relationship, and you do not. Your prospects, and people in general, feel more comfortable in a familiar, stable environment. As the advocate of change, you are the one who is introducing the uncertainty.

The Power of the Incumbent

On the second day of a selling workshop I was doing, a successful sales professional raised his hand. "Randy," he said, "I've just had an epiphany." When we realized we did not need to call a doctor, he explained what it was. "All my life I've been taught to go sell myself, to sell me. I believe I've got it backward. Before I start selling me, I need to unsell the current provider. Once I get them unsold and off the throne, then I can sell me."

That is the point. There is a throne, and only one person on it. To sell yourself and win the account, you have to kick the present provider off that throne and create the space you need. A current provider's position is so strong that it is almost as if the laws of physics were at work. What has Sir Isaac Newton got to do with this? If he were at your next sales meeting, I believe he would bring along at least three PowerPoint slides:

[*Click*] No Two Objects Can Occupy the Same Space at the Same Time

It is a pretty good rule of thumb that the more desirable an account, the more likely that someone already has it. You know this, for example, if you are a banker, or a wealth manager, or are with one of the Big Five consulting firms. When you go after a plum account, a rival will be occupying the space you want. He or she will be on the throne. As long as that is the case, since you cannot occupy it at the same time, you have to knock him or her off the throne before you can be in a position to win.

[*Click*] For Every Action, There Is an Equal and Opposite Reaction

I remember when I first got into selling. I was aggressive and had a desire to prove myself. I wanted to make something happen. At the very beginning of my sales career, I did what I always did when I was competing, as if I were playing football or basketball. I attacked my competitor. The problem was that the prospect would get defensive, and I would get thrown out of the office. If you want to make people defensive, it is easy. Just start talking negatively about the decisions they have made.

When I acknowledged that combat did not work, I started to play as if I had no competitor. Maybe you are like I was then, and you have made selling a solo sport. I would think, "Let me sell *me*, and everything will take care of itself. If I do enough, then at some point I'll get the business." My boss told me, "Selling is about relationships. Go build them. Get prospects to like you. Make a proposal. They can't make a decision if you don't give them a proposal. If you don't succeed the first time, try again. Go back the next year. If after a while you still don't have the business, maybe it was just a bad prospect." This thinking still influences many salespeople. It is causing them to inflict pain on themselves as they build prolonged relationships that go nowhere. It is stopping them from thinking differently, and being open to a new approach.

The reality is that there *is* a competitor. It is time to stop playing as if there is not. In this book, you are going to learn how to deal with that reality, take back control of the selling cycle, and make winning more predictable.

[*Click*] An Object at Rest Tends to Stay at Rest

As I mentioned before, many people today have lowered their expectations to what they are receiving, whether it's the way their spouse cooks green beans compared with the way their parent did, or the way they get treated when they visit the supermarket. Your prospect's relationship with his or her current provider is the same way. It is probably pretty good for the most part, and your prospect is reasonably happy. He or she accepts things as they are. And a relationship at rest, like an object at rest, tends to stay at rest.

The question is: How do you get your prospect to be unhappy? In fact, there is a lot of *latent* dissatisfaction among prospects. But how do you get your prospects to confront their dissatisfaction and do something about it? How do you get them to see clearly where they are being underserved, and to be motivated to take action? Your prospects' latent pain is the external force that you can use to disturb the object at rest, and get your prospects to pay attention.

You can tap into this pain not only if someone already

has the account, but also when you are competing for an open account.

Pain

Avoiding pain is a basic human motivation. I learned this myself at an early age, when I was growing up on a farm outside Lubbock, Texas. Like many of our neighbors, my family raised cows. We had one black Angus cow named Susie. She was a sweet old cow, but was hard to keep fenced in. So my dad, unknown to me, put up an electric fence. One day I went outside to feed the cows and, like always, was about to crawl through the barbed-wire fence when— *"Ouch!"* Man, I got hit with a bolt of lightning that almost knocked me down. It taught me not to do that again. Pain is one huge motivator.

We have learned from behavioral studies that about 65 to 70 percent of human motivation comes from avoiding pain, while only 30 to 35 percent comes from seeking pleasure. If you have been in sales for more than a week, this is probably a fairly obvious concept to you. The big challenge is taking the idea of finding pain from a concept to a reality. It is one of the biggest problems we have as salespeople. Because most of our prospects have lowered their expectations, they are satisfied, or at least content. We are all guilty of this. Think about your car, house, kids, spouse, job, commute, boss, parents, clothes, and the list can go on. For the most part, isn't it true that you are reasonably content with things because you have lowered your expectations down to what you have? This is the secret to how not to be miserable. It is the exact same thing that prospects are doing. That's why it is so difficult to find a telling need, pain, or dissatisfaction when we go on sales calls.

Here is another example. Just like you, I make sales calls. Many of my prospects have never thought about what it costs for their companies to produce quotes. To them, doing so is just part of the overhead. The way my business operates, it's remarkably different. It's an acquisition cost we watch. Many larger companies have some sort of staff to help estimate costs, write proposals, and format, copy, collate, and deliver them. Putting together proposals is a significant expense, but many of them write it off as just a cost of doing business. In other words, they have lowered their expectations down to what they are getting. They accept a certain amount of wasted expense. And many are getting low closing ratios, high sales costs, and mediocre profitability. What's my point? Finding pain is tough many times because our prospects have stuffed their expectations of having things be better in some storage bin, to be considered at a later time.

So here is the million-dollar question: How do you get your prospects to feel the dissatisfaction, frustration, disappointment, concern, anxiety, discomfort, or other negative emotional state that they could be feeling in regard to their current service? More important, how do you get them to blame this dissatisfaction, frustration, disappointment, concern, anxiety, or discomfort on your competitor, the incumbent? If you can tap into this pain, you can use its emotional power as the outside force to overcome the incumbent's natural advantage. Getting your prospect to feel pain is essential to winning business. Why? Because if no realization of a problem occurs, there is no solution—and you have nothing to sell.

One of the biggest pains of buyers is a lack of understanding about things that results in their having an inability to control their own future. Think about your own situation. Take the tax code, for example. On the one hand, you may fear that you will overpay. On the other hand, if you are too aggressive, you worry about triggering an Internal Revenue Service audit. Why don't you have better control over your future? Because the tax code is so complicated that who knows what might happen. Our lives are full of uncertainty about the things whose future we cannot control. What will your car or home be worth in five years? Are you in the right job? Will your products last? Will you get cancer? Your prospects are in the same situation. They think about the future of their business, and they realize that there are many things they cannot predict. Our job as salespeople is to help them stay in control of those things that are controllable, easing the pain they feel and making their future more predictable.

Your prospect's pain is the Newtonian outside force that you can use to break apart the otherwise unbreakable bond between your prospect and the current provider, and to gain an advantage over any competitor. This pain is what permits you to use The Wedge, the strategy and tactics that you are going to employ to get your competition fired.

Highlights

What have we learned so far?

- Most selling opportunities involve three parties—a seller, a buyer, and the seller's competition, the crucial third party overlooked in traditional selling strategies.
- By shifting your focus to the relationship between your prospect and the competition, you can stop selling and start winning.
- Just as you protect your own accounts from competitors, current providers will try to stop you from winning business from their clients.
- No two objects can occupy the same space at the same time. You must knock the present provider off his or her throne in order to win the business.
- For every action, there is an equal and opposite reaction. If you attack the provider, your prospect will get defensive and shut down.
- An object at rest tends to stay at rest. Most prospect-provider relationships are objects at rest, in part because prospects have lowered their expectations to the service they are currently receiving.
- Your prospect's pain regarding his or her current service is the outside force you can use either to break the prospect-provider relationship or to top your other competitors, and win the business. It is what permits you to use The Wedge to get your competition fired.

Factoring in the competition literally changes the way selling is done. The next chapter shows you how The Wedge will powerfully enhance your precall strategy and make winning more predictable. We look at how you can clearly differentiate yourself from competitors—matching your strengths against their weaknesses—and find your true competitive advantage. Once you have done this, you can tap into your prospects' pain and help them discover for themselves why they should be doing business with you.

As we move on, let me ask you this: Why *should* your prospect hire you and not your competitor? Exactly what makes you better?

CHAPTER

2

Finding Your Winning Difference

Remember the hit movie *Speed*? A bad guy played by Dennis Hopper secretly rigs a bus with a bomb. Once the bus is out on the open highway doing better than 50 miles per hour, Dennis phones his old nemesis, a SWAT team member played by Keanu Reeves, and gives Keanu the bad news: The instant the bus slows down below 50, *kaboom!*

If you are like a lot of hardworking salespeople I know, you are driving that bus and you have the pedal to the floor. Go, go, go. Hit the street. Make those calls. Send those follow-up e-mails. Generate those leads. Touch base with those accounts. Drop in on those prospects. Go to that reception. Keep at it. Keep plugging. You cannot slow down because if you do, *kaboom!* In your mind, every moment that you are not contacting prospects is a dangerous moment. Slow down now, and your career would blow up. But slow down you must, if you want to find your winning difference.

In this chapter, we look at how to do the kind of strategic precall research that will enable you to define your competitive advantage clearly and powerfully. If you are going to bust an existing relationship, then you need to go into your sales call prepared with the knowledge of why your prospect needs you, and how your prospect is being underserved by the current provider. If you are competing for an open account, you need the same clear picture of your strengths. You have to be able to get your prospects to acknowledge and understand *how* they are being underserved by your competitor and how they will be better served by you. Doing this kind of precall research will enable you to find the specific proactive services that you provide and your competition doesn't, and that will enable you to proactively control your prospects' experiences, making their future more predictable.

How, then, do you find and effectively articulate your competitive advantages—your winning difference?

Information, Knowledge, and Intelligence

The Internet has leveled the playing field when it comes to quickly finding out basic information about companies and what they do. Anyone who has heard of Google, Yahoo!, or MSN can check out most medium-sized and larger businesses without having to place a single phone call. For public companies, you can visit EDGAR (Electronic Data Gathering, Analysis, and Retrieval System) online at www.sec.gov and review its Securities and Exchange Commission filings, which are chock-full of useful information. Most companies of any size these days have some presence on the World Wide Web that is retrievable via search engines. With information no longer scarce, the research advantage in selling goes to those who can gain the insights and discover the specific critical facts unique to each situation. As others have noted, we are advancing from the "information age" to the "knowledge age."

There is a significant difference between the information that is readily available from public sources and the knowledge you must have to develop a winning strategy. There are many critical items you must know. As a salesperson, you know what these include. What are your prospect's strategic objectives? Who influences the buying decisions? If there is a current provider, how long has that person had the prospect's business? How did he or she get that business? Is the prospect just another customer of the provider, or do they have a closer relationship, more like partners? Has it been a rocky situation at times, or are they bosom buddies? Is there any scuttlebutt on problems or issues in the way service is being provided? The question is: How do you get this knowledge? Obviously, these are not the kinds of questions whose answers are posted on a company's web site. So this is where you use your interpersonal skills to make contacts and develop sources. If you have been in sales for any length of time, you already know how to do this and are reasonably good at it.

After moving from Web-based research for the information every salesperson has to Wedge-based research for the knowledge *you* need to begin creating the winning difference that will help you get the deal, you must then drill down even deeper into a third level of detail. Once you have the facts—the inside knowledge that you need about a prospect—you need to convert that knowledge into intelligence. In other words, you need to analyze what you know, convert it into the most powerful way that you can leverage it, and go into your sales call in a position to use that knowledge intelligently to maximize your competitive advantage.

Here is an example of what I mean. Let's say you found out that Holding Company of America was shopping advertising agencies to handle its retail clothing store chain. So you amassed information on the company, and then you dug deeper and found out that Holding felt its current agency had been less than aggressive in placing its TV advertising efficiently. Holding did not feel that it was getting the biggest bang for its buck. Obviously this is a key piece of knowledge. The question is: How can you most intelligently use that knowledge to your advantage? How can you leverage your proactive services to make Holding's future more predictable? It would make sense in this case for you to make Holding aware of your reporting system that spells out in detail the demographic groups targeted, the cost objective for reaching them, the audience actually reached, the cost efficiency of the buy based on a media audit, and a plan for how your media buyers will obtain and document bonus spots, make-goods, and other added value for Holding. That awareness will give Holding a clear picture, based on something real and concrete, of how you would ease its anxiety in a way that will also compare you favorably with Holding's current agency.

The question is: How do you do the kind of precall research to contrast yourself with your competition without saying anything bad about them, and in a way that leads your prospects to conclude on their own that they are being underserved and should be doing business with you?

Researching Your Competition

I have been amazed during my years as a consultant at the number of salespeople who research their prospect, get an appointment, go in and start presenting, and do not know who the current provider is, or who else is pitching the account. For the most part, it is not because they could not have found out. It is just that they had no reason to value doing it. Often, they were engaged in traditional selling as its best. They would create a relationship, ask a lot of questions, learn their prospect's needs, and work hard to identify problems for which they could offer solutions. They would operate by the book, the way consultative selling is supposed to work, between a seller and a buyer.

When these salespeople did undertake competitor research, it frequently was the type that gave them the kind of reconnaissance they could get from 30,000 feet up instead of the kind that would give them some traction on the ground.

I am going to show you a different way to do competitive research. Instead of spending your time boning up on the same stuff everyone else knows, you will be focusing on those things about your competition that will give you the edge you need to win the account. The purpose of research based on The Wedge is not to make you an expert on the competition. It is to identify the competition's vulnerabilities—the areas where your competition is already underserving your prospect, or would be if they were hired instead of you—and to use those areas of underservice to motivate your prospect to hire you instead of keeping or hiring them.

Why More Salespeople Don't Do the Right Kind of Research

Traditional selling, as we noted, takes competition for granted. It assumes that your relationship with the buyer is the key relationship for you to focus on, and that the issue of your competition will somehow take care of itself. But as you know, it does not really work that way. Many salespeople have developed great relationships with companies that never did end up giving them a contract. Pure relationship selling may be pleasant and enjoyable, but it is more a luxury for the rich than a tool for growing new business with any great degree of speed or predictability.

So why is it that more salespeople do not make researching their rivals a vital part of their precall preparation and strategy? For one thing, they target prospects that they know are looking, where there is no embedded incumbent to oust. They go into those sales calls, tell their stories, and hope for the best. Where there is active competition for an account or an incumbent in place, they feel the pressure of time. They question the value of using their limited time for competitor research. They don't know if it really helps all that much.

Many sales managers reinforce this type of thinking. They encourage their sales representatives to stay busy, make a lot of calls and contacts, and keep pitching. They are not trained to teach their reps how to get the knowledge they really need, how to contrast their proactive services with those of the competition in order to make a comparison that truly gives their reps something to sell. These sales managers cannot show their reps how to descend from 30,000 feet to the ground, and start winning in one-to-one combat.

Later on, in Chapter 8, I introduce a sales meeting format called CRISP (continuous and rapid improvement sales process). The idea is to convert your sales meeting into a catalyst for driving growth by focusing on the concrete, specific proactive services relevant to each prospect that will move the deal forward. As we have discussed, this is a critical element in winning. If you don't have a persuasive point of comparison with your competition based on proactive service, you very likely will never get the traction you need to get your competition fired.

The Research You Need to Win

As we discussed earlier, companies compete on price, product, and service. Usually a company will not find any sustainable competitive advantage in price—not unless it has chosen to hang its hat on price, as with retailers like Wal-Mart and Dell computers. Moreover, in services industries especially, CEOs are not happy to hear that their sales reps went out and doubled new business by beating the competition on price. And where price differences do exist between competitors, they are usually too marginal to be decisive. Similarly, product differences are usually either too slight or too short-lived to be sustained. Unless your company has an airtight patent, you can't count on milking a product advance for very long before your competitors start introducing something equivalent.

This leaves service, and most companies think that "great service" consists of being responsive to their customers' needs, of being there for them. The problem is that all companies say that. Who other than a monopoly can get away with not being responsive to its customers? Everybody does a decent job of reactive service. It's as basic to a company's survival as a cash balance and working telephones. It's a minimum for staying in the game, not a competitive advantage.

Competitive advantage comes from proactive service, the day-to-day things a company does to make its customers' future more predictable. These days, companies with a strong proactive services platform can make it their greatest differentiator in winning business away from competitors. By researching and comparing the proactive service you offer with the service your competition offers—and by matching your strengths against your competition's weaknesses regarding proactive service in order to find your competitive advantage—you can gain the knowledge you need to use The Wedge and to start winning more new business than you ever have.

Let me repeat the mantra, because it really is one of the central themes of this book: Our job as salespeople, the thing we need to do to make The Wedge work for us, is to proactively control the experiences of our clients, making their future more predictable.

Researching Yourself

In 1996, my consulting firm conducted a survey of insurance agencies across the United States. We asked each agency to tell us what it was saying about itself in its marketing. In other words, what made it different from (and better than) its competitors. When we compiled the results, we were struck by their uniformity. With almost no exception, every agency we contacted cited the same attributes:

competitive prices, great service, impeccable reputation, highly trained professional staff, years in business, and commitment to quality. Had we kept them on the phone longer, I am sure we would have heard about the friendly receptionist in the lobby and the nice plants in the atrium. What these agencies claimed made them better made them the same.

In most industries even today, many salespeople are trying to win accounts by citing things about their companies that merely reflect the minimum standard for remaining in business. Not surprisingly, the mediocre results they get reflect the minimum standard for remaining in sales. When you are selling parity, you are just one more sheep in the flock.

How, then, do you get at what makes you better? How do you drill down and find the things that will make your prospects clearly see why they should be doing business with you?

What Is Competitive Advantage?

Do you know your competitive advantage? Here is a simple definition: It is your strengths versus your competition's weaknesses. That is your competitive advantage.

When a provider already has the account, the advantage can be formidable. You are in a losing position that is difficult to overcome. Your competition has the account, and you do not. Imagine yourself in a game against the current provider. All that provider needs to do is tie, or maybe even score a little less than you. It already has the relationship with the prospect. It has home field advantage. It is the reigning champion, and you are the challenger who is trying to unseat the incumbent champion.

Every company has strengths and weaknesses—your company as well as your competition's company. To give yourself the best chance to win, you will need to have a good idea of which of your strengths match up favorably against your competition's weaknesses. When researching and comparing yourself with your competition, remember these three rules:

1. Your strength versus the competition's strength = tie, or you lose.
2. Your weakness versus the competition's strength = you lose.
3. Your strength versus the competition's weakness = you win.

Rule 3 is the only place you can find the advantages that you have over your competition. Do you know what your strengths are that might match up well against the weaknesses of your competition? If not, I would ask you: What do you have to sell?

How to Find Your Competitive Advantage

There are three ways you can have a competitive advantage in services. First, you can provide a service that is unique, that no one else provides. Second, you can provide a service that others provide, but you have a better process for it that gets better results. Third, you can describe the service you offer in such a clear and compelling way that prospects are motivated to buy from you rather than from your competitors.

Only You Do It

I was once conducting a workshop for a major financial services corporation that was having trouble articulating exactly what made it better than and different from its competitors. The company had a terrific brand, but its senior executives and sales managers could not readily come up with the specific strengths that differentiated the company from its rivals. During the course of the workshop, a woman who worked for the company spoke up as if to remind me to keep things in perspective. "Randy," she said, "our brand is worth $14 billion." "I know it is," I replied. "That gets you in the door, but it doesn't get you the deal."

A lot of your competitors have great brands, too. Most of the time, your brand versus another good brand is a wash. The question is: What do you have to sell? Do you have a service that only your company offers? If so, congratulations. Most companies do not have such an obvious, readily apparent competitive advantage. Even if they do, it likely will not last long—whether it is cell phones with pictures, extra leg room on a passenger jet, global positioning systems in rental cars, or customer change counters in bank lobbies. For differentiation that matters and lasts, you will most often need to look elsewhere rather than rely on your brand and your occasional innovations.

You Have a Better Process for It That Gets Better Results

My wife, Lori, and I celebrated our 15th wedding anniversary by treating ourselves to a stay at a five-star Dallas hotel. When we came down for breakfast in the morning, the maître d' welcomed us into the dining room. I was taken aback when I looked at the menu to discover that a basic scrambled egg breakfast was going to cost us $29.95 each. As politely as I could, I asked if there were an alternative breakfast place, and we were referred to a restaurant down the street that featured a $2.95 scrambled egg special. How was it that our five-star hotel, using the same eggs from Arkansas and the same city water, was able to serve up a meal that sold for 10 times more? Its chef had a better process that got better results. In one case, the eggs would turn out light, fluffy, and superbly palatable; and in the other place, where we decided to dine, they proved to be more like rubber bands.

When you and your competitors are offering identical or similar services, it is not merely *what* you do that makes you better but *how* you do it. In business, the question to ask yourself is: Where do I have better processes that produce better results, creating more predictable results for my clients? How do I drill down into the details to find them?

For example, there are about half a million certified public accountants (CPAs) in the United States. They all can do taxes. But *how* they do taxes varies. One might claim to minimize your tax liability but merely send you a completed return to sign. Another might stop by your office in December and go over a tax minimization checklist with you, looking for areas to reduce your liability and giving you other specific advice so that you do not overpay (a proactive service).

Suppose, for another example, that you own your own home, and your homeowner's insurance policy includes coverage of your personal property. You want to make sure you are protected, so you regularly write a check for the premium. But do you really know what is covered and what is

53

not? Some insurers simply provide the policy and the required explanatory documents. But wouldn't it be nice if your agent came out 60 days before renewal to do an exposure analysis, and went over a checklist to see what items you have bought such as cars, jewelry, furniture, and other add-ons to make certain everything was covered (a proactive service)?

Again we see that your competitive advantage lies not only in *what* you do but also in *how* you do it. This is where you can find your better process that gets better results, and creates more predictable results for your clients.

Nowhere are the opportunities greater for you to create competitive advantage than in the proactive services you provide. These are the specific, concrete things you do to make your client's future more predictable.

I recommend to my own clients that they create a *written proactive services time line* for each of their customers. The time line sets forth the things they will do in the course of the year to provide service, prevent problems, deal in a timely fashion with issues that arise, and otherwise make life more predictable and more successful for the people who have hired them. By putting a written proactive services time line in place, they are making their service more predictable for their clients in areas where their clients previously were underserved. This helps prevent new pain from jeopardizing their current relationship with their clients, and it also "Wedge-proofs" these clients by making their service predictable.

You Differentiate It Compellingly

How many times have you spoken to a "computer person," a technical person in information technology (IT), and carried on an understandable, meaningful dialogue that enabled you simply and easily to grasp the main points? Indeed, how many times have you had a conversation with an IT person that lasted more than 30 seconds? For most of us, computer people have a language all their own that defies our immediate understanding.

The challenge for nearly all businesspeople is that each of us has a language peculiar to our own industry that prospects do not fully understand. This creates a major selling problem. What prospects do not understand they cannot appreciate. If we are unable to translate the value of what we do into clear, concrete examples that prospects understand, then we cannot gain a competitive advantage from that value. I ask you again: If you cannot articulate your competitive advantage, what do you have to sell?

What happens is that you end up relying on pure relationship selling. You develop trust and comfort with your prospect, and hope to be there when the opportunity to win business arises. But would it not be better to shorten the time it takes to get paid, to have a predictable way of winning new business without having to rely on relationships that may or may not quickly bear fruit? That is what this book is about. Your strategy using The Wedge is to go in there and bust the relationship between your prospect and the current provider. How can you best do that? By helping your prospects see in the clearest, most concrete way possible how they are being underserved by their provider, or would be without you. That is the way to create truly powerful differentiation, gain competitive advantage, shorten the selling cycle, and win the account.

The Ladder of Abstraction

What does "quality" look like? Can you draw a picture of "love"? If you cannot, neither can your prospect. If your prospect is unable to visualize what you are offering, how will he or she be able to comprehend a meaningful difference between you and your competitors? Yet this is the way too many salespeople try to differentiate themselves. They have a mental thesaurus full of glittering generalities—great prices, dependable quality, friendly service, real value, blah, blah, blah!

You may remember the late U.S. Senator S.I. Hayakawa. He was a mustachioed politician and academic who was partial to wearing tams. In the late 1960s, as president of what was then San Francisco State College, Hayakawa took a stand against the disruptive tactics of unruly student protestors. But Hayakawa's first passion was language, not politics or grating on rebellious young people. In his book *Language in Thought and Action*, Hayakawa wrestled with the way we use words to convey meaning. He put the language we use on a scale, from abstract to concrete. He called his scale "the ladder of abstraction." The lower on the ladder, the more concrete the word. The higher on the ladder, the more abstract the word.

Abstract/General versus Concrete/Specific

My daughter, Reagan, brought home from school an excellent example of the ladder of abstraction. It was a chart showing how dairy products are organized in a supermarket. Imagine Reagan's chart as a ladder. On the top rung is the word "dairy."

However, if you asked your spouse to pick up some "dairy" on the way home from the office, the term would not be very useful. On the next rung down are the words "milk" and "cheese," dividing dairy products into these two broad categories. Again, unless you had no real food preferences, asking your spouse for "milk" or "cheese" would not necessarily enable you to get what you wanted. Moving further down the ladder, the "milk" products are divided into skim, 1 percent, 2 percent, whole, and half-and-half; and the "cheese" products are divided into American, Swiss, cheddar, cream cheese, and cottage cheese. Moving still lower on the ladder, the specific kinds of cheese are further broken down into, for example, various degrees of fat and sodium content. Now we are talking. "Honey, could you pick up some low-fat, small-curd cottage cheese on the way home?"

Selling on the Lower Rungs

The ladder of abstraction can be applied to any product or service you offer. At some point as you work your way down the ladder, the concreteness and specificity of what you are talking about become clear to your prospect. That is why it is more effective to sell from the lower rungs of the ladder—where you and your prospect have the same mental picture, and you therefore can get your prospect to appreciate *how* you do things better. When you have done that, you can leverage your competitive advantage over the competition.

Consider our earlier examples in light of the ladder of abstraction.

Remember the major financial services corporation

with the $14 billion brand that could not articulate its differentiation from competitors? Once we started moving down the ladder of abstraction in our workshop, it turned out that this company had a specific way of training its clients that enabled those clients to get more value from their relationships than they could with similar financial services firms that provided comparable training. That specific, concrete difference in the method of training proved to be a marketable point of differentiation that enabled the company to use The Wedge to win business away from its competitors.

When choosing between the two CPAs who both offer to minimize your tax liability, would you rather have one who fulfills that promise by merely mailing you a completed tax return to sign or one who stops by your office in December and goes over a tax minimization checklist to make sure everything is considered?

When choosing between the two homeowner's insurance providers who both cover your tangible personal property, would you rather have one who merely mails premium renewal notices, or one who is willing to stop by your house 60 days before renewal to make sure any newly acquired items are covered?

In each case, while the promised benefit is the same, one company has a better process that produces better results, and by staying low on the ladder of abstraction the company can communicate to you in concrete terms *how* it is better than its competitors.

Where to Look

Where do you look to find the concrete things you do on a day-to-day basis that you can get your prospect to visualize? Where do you find the corresponding weaknesses on the part of the competition? Where do you find the material for the sound bites that create visuals contrasting your strengths with the competition's weaknesses?

I can give you the techniques to use so that you can come up with the specific examples that fit your situation. First, you need to put yourself in the shoes of your prospects. Ask yourself what would typically be some of the things they dislike. These are the areas where you can develop proactive solutions. In most industries, salespeople have a pretty good idea of what these pain-producing problems are likely to be. A generic list of painful symptoms to tell you where to look more deeply might include such complaints as:

- I never see our rep.
- My calls are not returned quickly.
- The invoices were higher than we expected.
- They do not seem to really understand our business.
- They do not bring us new ideas and suggestions unless we ask.
- They give us things at the last minute.
- Our billings are inaccurate.
- Things seem to fall between the cracks.

Just about any business should have 12 to 18 specific, concrete examples of service strengths (such as those that match up against your competitors' service weaknesses related to the symptoms just cited) that it can use the ladder of abstraction to communicate effectively to its prospects.

Winning with Precision and Confidence

When you have found your winning differences, and know how to communicate them powerfully by staying low on the ladder of abstraction, you will be able to go into any selling situation with more precision in finding the pain that will drive The Wedge, and with greater confidence of winning.

During the first Gulf War following Saddam Hussein's occupation of Kuwait, television viewers were awed by the accuracy of the munitions. Laser-guided missiles were literally sent down the chimneys of buildings or through front doors. One bomb, one successful hit. It was in sharp contrast to the tactics of World War II, when multiple bombs were often scattered over a broad area to increase the odds of hitting a target. The Wedge is efficient in the same way. When you have the specific, concrete examples you need to find your prospect's pain, you can use your time far more productively—getting to the heart of the matter without a lot of peripheral discussion.

At your next sales meeting, you can benefit greatly by putting your prospects, your competitors, and your own company up there on the whiteboard, drilling down into what makes you better than and different from your competitors, matching that up with your prospects' likely pain, and then converting those examples into concrete chunks that you can go out and use to create the kind of powerful differentiation you need to drive The Wedge between your prospects and your competitors.

Because you know the details, you and your colleagues will go into selling situations with more confidence—no more relying on generalities that result in follow-up questions you cannot answer. When you think about it, there are four levels of knowing: you either know something; you know about something, you do not know it; or you do not know that you do not know it. One of the keys to rapid growth is to stop faking knowledge. Admit what you do not know, and then learn it as rapidly as possible. Differentiation using the ladder of abstraction to find the concrete, specific things that are your competitive advantages will enable you to pursue new business based on what you actually do know. Knowledge is power and, in selling, knowledge gives you the confidence you need to win the respect of your prospects.

Summary

Before we move ahead and discuss how to conduct a sales call using The Wedge, let us take a moment to review the highlights of this chapter:

- Your precall research should include all three parties in the selling situation—your prospect, the competition, and yourself.

- Your research should focus on finding and clearly describing your competitive advantages over the competition related to the pain your prospect is likely to have regarding the current provider's service. The better and different service that you can offer to ease your prospect's pain, contrasted with the prospect's current service that is causing that pain, is your winning difference.

- The specific *knowledge* you can gain about a company from individual people in the know can have much more impact than the vast amount of *information* available via the Internet and other media. Your next step is to use that knowledge with *intelligence*, converting it into a form that will enable you to powerfully state your competitive advantage.

- Questions to address when researching prospects include: Who will make the decision to hire me, and who influences that decision? If there is a current provider, what is the nature of the provider's relationship with the prospect, including any weaknesses in service and other areas of vulnerability? Whom do I know who knows someone who works for the prospect?

- When researching the competition and your own company, you should look for your strengths that match up favorably against the competition's weaknesses. Those are your competitive advantages.

- There are basically three dimensions of competition: price, product, and service. Your greatest opportunity to gain competitive advantage and win accounts lies in service, and especially in proactive service, not reactive service.

- There are three places you can find your competitive advantage in services: (1) something that only you do; (2) something that you and others do, but you have a better process for doing it that gets better results; and (3) something that you and others do, but you have a compelling way of describing it that motivates prospects to want to do business with you.

- It is not just *what* you do but *how* you do it that makes you better. In explaining how you do something, you should identify and communicate the specific things that you do, rather than giving your prospect general descriptions.

- When talking to prospects, stay low on the *ladder of abstraction*, using concrete, specific words that create mind pictures.

- You should create for each prospect and client a *proactive services time line*. This time line will prevent the pain your prospect associates with his or her current service, and will help to ensure continuing client satisfaction with you.

- Your job as a salesperson is to proactively control the experiences of your clients, making their future more predictable.

- By doing precall research that matches your strengths against the competition's weaknesses, that enables you to compellingly describe your proactive services in concrete terms that differentiate you from the competition, and that prompts your prospects to conclude that doing business with you will alleviate the pain they associate with their current service, you can begin winning new business more predictably.

Now that you have learned The Wedge precall strategy, it is time to examine the tactics that you can use to win the account by getting your competition fired . . . without saying anything bad about them.

Part II outlines a six-step conversation, The Wedge Sales Call, that you can use as a format each time you visit with a prospect. It is not a script, something you need to memorize. It is a conversational road map, with easy-to-remember segue phrases to take you from one step to the next.

Your approach in using The Wedge to win new business will no longer be to "sell" prospects. You are going to leave traditional selling behind—no more canned presentations, feature benefit spiels, and trial closes. Instead, you will guide your prospects through a process of self-discovery, letting them stay comfortably in control of the pace. When you have done it right, your prospects will ask *you* to do business, and they will affirm that they are ready to fire their provider, or to stop talking to your competitors, in order to hire you and make it happen.

PART

II

THE TACTICS THAT WORK

The Wedge Sales Call

In the original Indiana Jones movie, *Raiders of the Lost Ark*, Harrison Ford is confronted by a menacing figure who pulls out a sword, putting it through a series of ominous gyrations and flourishes until Ford, unimpressed by the villain's dexterity, casually grabs a pistol from his own holster and brings an abrupt end to the performance.

There is a reason many prospects are similarly impatient as they sit through sales presentations. In the traditional selling process, there are two people—you and your prospect. The sales call is about your ability to create rapport, know your prospect, and ask questions to find out where he or she has pain. Traditional selling assumes that your prospects will know where they hurt, and will tell you. You then fashion a solution for their pain, make a proposal, overcome any objections that are raised, and move to close the deal. Traditional selling is a workable process. Many billions of dollars' worth of services and products have been sold using it. But too often it ends short of a deal. Your prospect, figuratively reaching for his or her holster like Harrison Ford, pulls out a revolver at the end of your presentation and fires the fatal shot: "Let me think about it."

Why does traditional selling fall short so often? I believe that there are two key reasons:

First, as we have discussed, traditional selling does not deal with your competition. Because of this, when you use traditional selling methods, your focus is not on beating your competition. Moreover, if your prospect has a provider, there is a great chance that the provider will be able to leverage his or her relationship with the prospect, match your deal, and keep the business. This helps explain why, in many industries, providers enjoy such a high retention rate with their clients. Traditional selling does not recognize that for you to win someone has to lose.

Second, traditional selling assumes that most buyers know where they hurt. One of my core beliefs is that they do not. They have lowered their expectations down to what they are receiving and are getting what they now expect to be getting. When you ask these prospects how things are going, they will say "fine." When you ask them if they have any problems, they will say "not really." Until you can raise their expectations, thereby creating pain, you have nothing to sell them.

Unlike traditional selling, The Wedge is about going into your sales call already knowing where your prospect is being underserved by the current provider, or is likely feeling pain due to a situation that you can address better than your competitors can. It is about getting your prospect to feel that pain so that you can drive The Wedge between your prospect and your competition.

This part of the book walks you through the six steps of The Wedge Sales Call. We will look at how each step works, and why. You will learn simple yet powerful phrases that you can use in your conversation with your prospects to guide them smoothly into inviting you to do business and affirming that they will fire their provider or dismiss your other competitors from consideration in order to hire you.

First, however, we are going to take a look at how you

create rapport with your prospects. Again, some of this will sound familiar to you. However, we are going to deal with rapport through the lens of The Wedge. The purpose of creating initial rapport during The Wedge Sales Call is more than simply to make your prospect comfortable with you. Your purpose is to foster the open, honest dialogue required for The Wedge to work.

Barriers to Rapport

It is a safe assumption that every account you seek is wanted or already handled by someone else. If there is a current provider, he or she already has rapport with your prospect. The provider and your prospect long ago got past their primary tension. By now, they speak in shorthand, communicating ideas back and forth with no need to get the preliminaries out of the way first. You, on the other hand, are the outsider. The provider has the relationship, and you do not. Moreover, even if the account is open, your prospect has likely been wooed by your competitors. Therefore, you are courting someone who either already has a significant other or at a minimum has been asked out on a date.

As we have discussed, your prospects have several reasons not to be completely truthful and candid with you when you walk in the door. For example, they may be shoppers with no intention to buy. They may have extended you the courtesy of presenting just so they could find out what is available in the market. Moreover, your prospect may have a current provider whom he or she hired. By being there, you are challenging a previous decision your prospect made. Even if the provider has flaws, no one likes to be told by someone else that he or she made a wrong decision.

Also, most prospects, like the majority of people, want to treat other people nicely. You may have gotten in to see the prospect for this very reason, in which case your reward will be a pleasant conversation and a free cup of coffee. Or it could be that you and your prospect just did not click when you walked in the door. The chemistry did not work; and your prospect has decided to simulate interest, hiding his or her personal displeasure behind a polite facial expression.

How, then, do you overcome these barriers and create the rapport you need to have an open, honest dialogue so that you can move the conversation into the six steps of The Wedge Sales Call?

Comfort and Credibility

To create an environment for truth telling, you must pass two tests. Fail either of them, and you can pretty much write off the sales call as a loss. The first of these is the comfort test. You have to make your prospect feel comfortable in your presence. The second of these is the credibility test. Your prospect needs to have confidence that you know what you are talking about, that you have what it takes to address his or her needs, and that you are a straight shooter who speaks honestly.

In his book, *Instant Rapport*, industrial psychologist

Michael Brooks discusses rapport as a technique that can be learned, a way of behaving that is not merely a talent of born salespeople. The point is that there are tactics you can use to create an environment in which your prospects are willing to tell you the truth. Why are they willing to be truthful? Because they are comfortable with you, and you are credible to them. You have met their need for someone they can talk to about their problems, and who can do something about those problems.

While it is true that communication is a two-way street, the burden for establishing the rapport is on you. You cannot rely on your prospect to break the ice and be a good host. This is a sales call, not a social visit to someone's house. It is you who wants something. And so it is your responsibility to make your prospect feel at ease.

When in Rome

I once had a meeting with a prospect about 25 years my senior. We were having breakfast in a Dallas hotel, and I was doing my best to make him comfortable. He was an easygoing fellow with a Texas drawl and a slow manner of speaking, so I slowed my own speech to match his, and sat back in my chair with a relaxed posture. As we kept talking, I realized my firm had the chance to win a $700,000 contract. The more I thought about the $70,000 fee that contract would generate, the more excited I got. I leaned forward eagerly, and started talking faster. It took me a while to recognize that his body posture had shifted. He had leaned back in his chair, crossed his legs, and turned 45 degrees away from me. He seemed to be signaling me to back off. In my zeal, I had created disharmony between us. He was protecting himself from the pressure I was creating. He was still laid-back, and I was wired, stimulated by coffee and thinking about that $70,000 fee. My unrestrained enthusiasm darn near killed the deal. Fortunately, I caught myself, sat back in my chair, crossed my legs, and slowed way down. We were back in sync, and the rapport was restored. (Yes. We got the contract.)

We have all heard the expression, "When in Rome, do as the Romans do." This does not mean that you have to become a chameleon and submerge your own identity. However, you can do a number of things to match and mirror your prospects' style, making them more comfortable. You can dress similarly, talk at the same speed, assume the same posture, and otherwise mirror their manner and temperament. Generally, people like people who are like themselves. Getting your prospect to relate to you is an important step in building the rapport you need to create the open, honest dialogue that will enable you to use The Wedge successfully.

Rapport can be conscious or subconscious. For example, if you see a picture on your prospect's desk of himself or herself skiing down the slopes at Aspen, you can ask when it was taken and mention how much you enjoy skiing yourself. Or you might point out that the iPod you spot on the desk is the same one that you have. Even though your conscious gesture is obvious, it is a friendly way to create some commonality at the beginning. From there, you can begin building a subconscious rapport by matching and mirroring in the manner previously described. You can adjust your talking speed, tone of voice, and body language to that of your prospect. These comfort-building tactics can go a long way toward encouraging your prospects to open up and share their real goals and concerns with you. They help create a willingness on your prospects' part to talk about what really matters to them. And when your prospects begin frankly sharing their thoughts and feelings with you, you can move the conversation to the matter at hand with a much greater chance of winning the business.

Tell a Story

Your prospects may be highly comfortable with you, but are you credible? That is, do your prospects have confidence that you can solve their problems? Do they believe you are a well-informed, honest person who knows their business? They might think you are a nice person, but not the one for the job. And you cannot *tell* your prospects that you are credible. People who make this claim invite suspicion. You cannot create credibility by sprinkling your conversation with phrases like "believe me," "call Bruce if you want confirmation," and "I've been there and done that." Your challenge is to get your prospects to conclude on their own that you are credible. One of the best ways I have found to do that is to tell a story.

By story, I mean a well-rehearsed account of a third party in a situation similar to that of your prospect. By recounting for your prospect how you helped this other party solve his or her problem, you are able to establish your own bona fides without sounding as if you are reciting bullets from a sales brochure. Here is a six-step format that you can use to tell your story:

1. *"You know, Susan, I've found in working with other companies like yours that . . ."* [Show her you know her industry and its market.]

2. *"The owner of one of these companies, Richard Green of Amalgamated Services, was concerned about . . ."* [Tell her about a specific problem like hers that you were able to solve.]

3. *"When I spoke to Richard, he told me what he wanted was . . ."* [Identify the desired solution in concrete, specific terms.]

4. *"So we went to work, and we were able to . . ."* [Explain how you gave Amalgamated that solution.]

5. *"As a result, Amalgamated achieved . . ."* [Quantify and describe the benefits that resulted.]

6. *"Tell me, Susan, about your situation . . ."* [Find out what she needs.]

On the surface, you have told Susan a story matter-of-factly, without hype and sales jargon. That was the *text* of your story. But the *subtext* of your story, the underlying message you were sending to Susan, was more assertive.

1. *Look, Susan. We know your business, your industry, and your market.*

2. *I've worked with people like you at the C level on problems like yours.*

3. *You can tell me your problem, and I'll get it fixed.*

4. *We can give you the same solutions we gave Amalgamated.*
5. *You're going to get measurable benefit from this.*
6. *Let's get started now on getting the job done.*

By conveying your strengths indirectly through a story, you have let Susan draw her own conclusions. You gave her a clear and specific example to think about—one that demonstrated your own capabilities and related them to her situation.

Summary

Before we move ahead to each of the steps of The Wedge Sales Call, let's review what we have just covered:

- Traditional selling often does not work because (1) it does not factor in the seller's competition, and (2) it assumes that buyers know where they hurt.

- In reality, (1) your sales success often depends on how you deal with your competitors, including current providers who have the power to match your offer and keep the business; and (2) most prospects have lowered their expectations to the level of service they are currently receiving, pushing their pain to the back of their mind. Buyers often do not know where they hurt.

- Unlike traditional selling, The Wedge Sales Call enables you (1) to get your prospects to see clearly where they are being underserved, and (2) to raise your prospects' expectations above their current level of service, creating the pain that you need in order to have something to sell them—and it enables you to accomplish both of these objectives without saying anything bad about your competition or having to sell yourself.

- For The Wedge Sales Call to work, you must create a rapport with your prospect so that you can have an open, honest dialogue.

- To achieve rapport with your prospect, you must pass two tests—comfort and credibility.

- You can make your prospect comfortable by matching and mirroring his or her temperament and style, and by finding common ground.

- You can gain credibility with your prospect by telling a story about a third party you helped whose situation was similar to that of your prospect. This enables you to establish your strengths and relate them to your prospects' needs without having to assert them directly and invite skepticism.

Now let me ask you something. What if you had a simple way of phrasing questions that made your prospects see how they were being underserved without your having to say anything bad about your competition? What if you could get your prospects to see how great you are without your having to tell them? What if you could quickly measure your prospects' pain to see whether it is strong enough for them to switch their business to you? What if you had a way to get your prospects to invite you in and ask you to do business with them? And what if you could get your prospects to confirm for you that they are ready and willing to hire you, even if it means firing your competition?

If you could accomplish these things during a relatively brief sales call, thus reducing the time it takes for you to win new business, would you be interested in hearing more?

That is what I am going to show you next—how to take your prospects through the six steps of The Wedge Sales Call. Learn these steps, and you can start winning more new business than you ever have.

CHAPTER 4

Discovering the Pain—
The Problem Phase

The Wedge Sales Call is a departure from traditional selling. Some salespeople take to it with alacrity and gusto. Others find it difficult at first to shake old habits. Some of the sales professionals I have coached carry around a card in their pocket listing the six steps, until they no longer need a cheat sheet. What nearly all these people have in common is that they are getting results using The Wedge—results that are repeatable from one prospect to the next, putting their performance on a new and higher trajectory.

Unlike traditional selling, The Wedge Sales Call is designed with the competition factored in at every step, from precall research to the time the deal is signed and under contract. As we have discussed, The Wedge also is based on concrete, specific differentiation that focuses on your strengths versus the competition's weaknesses.

Because The Wedge is about your helping your prospect come up with the solution rather than presenting a solution to your prospect, it enables you to prevent objections instead of having to overcome them. In a very real sense, The Wedge is more like education than selling. The root word of education is *educe*, to draw out. This is the very opposite of presentation. The more you help your prospects educate themselves as opposed to presenting to them, the greater your chance of winning their business.

In short, The Wedge works. Since my clients started using it, their success in many cases has been remarkable.

The Seven Rules of The Wedge

The Wedge Sales Call is based on human nature. As we have discussed, it was distilled from the experience of salespeople dealing with prospects. It is not a model reflecting how a seller and a buyer *should* behave, but a set of techniques to deal with how people *actually* behave. Its steps are intended to move the sales process forward to closure naturally, in a way that makes prospects feel as comfortable and in control as possible. Unlike traditional selling with its "gotcha" moment at which the salesperson does a trial close or flat out asks for the business, The Wedge Sales Call is a smooth, seamless conversation.

The Wedge Sales Call, to accommodate how people actually behave, takes into account these seven rules that govern human behavior:

1. *No two objects can occupy the same space at the same time.*

   As previously noted, if your prospect has a relationship with someone whose place you want to take, then you must first remove that person in order to fully take over the relationship. Even if an account is open, you must keep your competitors out of the space that you need to occupy to win.

2. *Nothing is either good or bad except by comparison.*

   This is a critical aspect of differentiation. In order to get your prospects to see how they are being underserved, you must present a picture of ideal service that creates a big enough gap between the ideal service and their current service to cause pain. This is

81

what makes the difference meaningful. This is what gives you something to sell.

3. *It is easier to get someone to deny perfection than it is to get them to admit to a problem.*

   When you are talking to prospects, it is better to get them to see an ideal service they do not have than to directly suggest that they have a problem to solve. Getting them to see the ideal will motivate them to want it. Suggesting that they have a problem of their own doing will put them on the defensive or, at a minimum, cause them to feel uneasy and pressured.

4. *The easiest way to get someone defensive is to talk negatively about a decision they have made.*

   This is why directly attacking a current provider is not a useful sales tactic. It merely puts your prospect on the defensive for having hired the provider. Nor should you speak negatively of your other competitors, as this makes prospects feel uneasy.

5. *The more you push people, the more they will push back to get even.*

   No one likes to be pushed into a corner with no way out. Their natural reaction is to push back, and to at least restore the equilibrium of their relationship with you.

6. *The best idea people ever heard was the one they thought of themselves.*

   Letting people discover their own solutions, as opposed to telling them what they should do, more powerfully commits them to those solutions. Remember your own resistance as a teenager when your parents told you what you *should* do? When you help your prospects discover their own solution, they will take ownership of it and feel more comfortable inviting you to help them achieve what *they* thought of.

7. *To gain leverage, never ask for the sale unless it is absolutely unavoidable. Make the prospect ask you.*

When you ask for business, you are putting your fate in the hands of the prospect, who can easily say yes or no. When you are asked in by a prospect, you have the power.

The most effective sales call is one that resembles a conversation between two friends, as opposed to a negotiation between a buyer and a seller. The Wedge Sales Call, embodying these seven rules, is designed to promote that kind of dialogue.

The Six Steps of The Wedge Sales Call

From this point forward, I use descriptive names for each step of The Wedge Sales Call. These labels are intended to capture the essence of each step. Let me lay out the whole structure for you, and then we will go through The Wedge Sales Call step by step. First, here is an outline of everything from start to finish:

Discovering the Pain (The Problem Phase)
    Step 1—PICTURE PERFECT
    Step 2—TAKE AWAY

Proposing a Remedy (The Solution Phase)
    Step 3—VISION BOX
    Step 4—REPLAY

Getting Your Competition Fired (The Commitment Phase)
    Step 5—WHITE FLAG
    Step 6—REHEARSAL

This chapter takes you through the first phase of The Wedge Sales Call. It is called the Problem Phase because, together, you and your prospect define the problem that needs to be fixed—the pain that needs to be removed. First, I show you how to get your prospect to discover his or her pain, using the PICTURE PERFECT technique. Then I show you how, using the TAKE AWAY, you can determine whether that pain is important enough to motivate your prospect to hire you by firing the current provider, or by dismissing your other competitors from consideration.

Chapter 5 looks at the Solution Phase. During this phase, you and your prospect agree on the specific, concrete remedy for your prospect's pain. First, I show you how to get your prospect to precisely define the solution that he or she wants, using the VISION BOX. Next, we look at how you can confirm that you understand the desired solution by using the REPLAY.

Chapter 6 explains the two steps of the Commitment Phase, the final part of The Wedge Sales Call, during which you get your prospect to commit to doing business with you. First, I show you how you can get your prospect to invite you to do business by using the WHITE FLAG.

Then we go over how, using the REHEARSAL technique, you can get your prospect to fire the current provider or to break the bad news to your other competitors in order to hire you.

To begin, then, let's take a look at the first two steps—PICTURE PERFECT and TAKE AWAY—exploring how and why they work.

Step 1: Picture Perfect

If you are like most salespeople I know, the most rewarding part of your job is helping people. What better way to make a living could there be than getting paid to make a positive difference for your prospects? That is why you went into sales—in addition to the fact that it pays very well if you are good at it.

Using The Wedge, you are going to do something even better for your prospects. You are going to help them help themselves. It is one thing to talk your prospects into accepting services and products that will yield *some* benefit, marginal or otherwise. It is quite another to help your prospects discover their most important needs, allowing you to focus your effort on helping them meet those needs.

Remember the question I asked earlier? What if you had a way to get your prospects to see how they are being underserved without your having to say anything bad about your competition, and to get them to see how great you are without your having to say it? I am now going to show you how to do that using PICTURE PERFECT.

Where Pain Resides

Finding pain is the turning point of a sales call. It is where you stop merely presenting and shift your focus to winning. Pain, you will recall, is the outside force you will use to break apart the relationship between your prospect and your competition. Pain is your means of driving The Wedge. Firing providers or dismissing others from consideration involves some discomfort on the part of your prospect. It is up to you to help your prospect see that the pain of telling someone good-bye is less than the pain of continuing to tolerate mediocre service.

Your role in finding pain is similar to that of a detective looking for clues. Just as a detective knows where to look for clues at a crime scene, your precall research has given you some good ideas of where to look for pain. And just as a detective knows how to interrogate suspects and witnesses, you will use questions to uncover any dissatisfaction, frustration, concern, anxiety, unresolved issue, or other discomfort your prospect is feeling.

To understand where pain resides, think of your brain as a computer. On your computer screen at any given time are up to half a dozen open windows. Think of these as the thoughts you currently have at the front of your mind. These thoughts represent your active memory—in the same way that the open windows on your computer screen represent the immediate activity of the central processing unit (CPU) of your computer. If you try to open too many windows at once on your computer screen, little gremlins come out, your computer locks up, and you suddenly blurt out colorful expressions. Your

86

mind works the same way. Most people can handle only six or seven active thoughts at one time before they hit overload.

Fortunately, your brain also has a storage bin—a rather vast one at that. It has enough capacity to house the thoughts, memories, and feelings of your entire lifetime. If your mind were a computer, this storage bin would be your hard drive. It contains billions of bytes of information. All that data sits there in ready reserve, waiting to be called up and into your active memory by the CPU as soon as someone makes the right keystroke.

These keystrokes are the questions people ask, and the things they do, that pull something from your latent memory into your active memory.

When you meet with your prospects, they may have an *active* pain that was obvious to them even before you arrived on the scene, or they might have a *latent* pain that they have stored in the back of their mind related to something they know needs to be done but that they have not addressed and fixed. They might even have a *potential* pain that does not exist at all—yet—because they have no idea that something could be done any better. Whatever its form, this pain is essential to winning business. If no realization of a problem occurs, there is no solution—and you have nothing to sell.

When you walk into your prospects' offices, they have a lot on their minds. Their active memories are going to be full. They may have a copy of the new financial quarterly report on their blotter. They may be looking at the sleeve of their fresh white dress shirt or blouse that they have just spilled coffee on. Today might be their anniversary or their child's birthday. Or maybe they just got off the phone with the current provider or one of your other competitors. You are going to be competing for their attention. In fact, most of the pain you are going to discover does not reside in your prospects' active memories. It is buried in their latent memories. Therefore, you are going to use your questioning skills to prompt your prospects to retrieve that pain, and to feel it actively.

Why is most pain buried in the back of prospects' minds? Obviously, from moment to moment, there is no room for that pain in the front of their minds. They have six or seven other things monopolizing their immediate attention. But there is another reason that runs deeper, and that explains why so much pain lies dormant for such a long time.

Think about how you react to a problem. You do one of two things: Either you solve it or you set it aside to solve later. If you solve it, the problem disappears and you file it away as finished business. If you do not solve the problem, it is because you were distracted by something else or because you could find no immediate solution. In that case, you store the problem in your latent memory as unfinished business. In other words, for every problem that arises, you either fix it or forget it.

This goes back to what I said before about expectations. Most prospects have forgotten their pain because they have come to accept their current level of service. They have reduced their expectations down to what they are receiving. Their pain lies dormant. Until you can get them to bring that pain to the surface, raising their expectations that things can be better, you have nothing to sell them. Traditional selling does not directly address how you can do this. The Wedge does.

Asking Questions That Uncover Pain

When you ask your prospect questions, your goal is to tap into your prospect's latent or active pain. Since you have done your precall research, you should have some idea of where to find your prospect's pain. Similar prospects are likely to have similar pain. Problems tend to repeat themselves within the same kinds of businesses and industries. So you should find it progressively easier to develop the right questions to elicit pain as you call on more prospects in your particular industry.

Regardless of the industry, the structure of the question is the same. Here is the question you are going to ask to get your prospect to focus on his or her pain:

> *"I'm curious. When you receive* [a specific service] *so that you don't have to worry about* [a specific pain], *are you comfortable with that process?"*

The question you have just asked is the PICTURE PERFECT question. You have painted a picture of the ideal service your prospect should be receiving. The structure of the question is simple in order to keep things conversational—but the question is powerful in the way it addresses the two key problems not addressed by traditional selling that we mentioned earlier. First, you are bringing up an ideal service that your competition is not offering or the current provider is not delivering. However, rather than attacking your competition, you are assuming that he or she does a good job. Second, you are getting your prospect to feel the pain of not currently receiving the PICTURE PERFECT service you just described. Now you have something to sell. Now you can use your prospect's pain to start driving The Wedge.

You have just taken the first step toward getting your competition fired or dismissed from consideration—and you did it without saying anything bad about your competitor. You gave your competition the benefit of the doubt. You assumed, in the question you asked your prospect, that the current provider was already delivering the ideal level of service, and that your other competitors could provide it. At the same time, you got your prospect to focus on his or her pain. You did this because pain avoidance (eliminating the problem) is a more powerful motivator than pleasure seeking (wanting the particular benefit).

PICTURE PERFECT is a powerful technique because, like The Wedge itself, it is based on human nature. Remember the third rule of The Wedge Sales Call? It is easier to get someone to deny things are perfect than it is to get them to admit there is a problem. When you ask a PICTURE PERFECT question, you are creating a conflict between the prospect and your competition. You are showing the prospect the gap between an example of ideal service and his or her current service. And you are doing it in a way that does not put your prospect on the spot. You are leaving it to your prospect to make the comparison and see the difference. You are not asking your prospect to admit there is a problem. You are only asking him or her to react by denying that things are as perfect as you portrayed.

90

Another salesperson might have said to your prospect, *"You are receiving* [a specific service] *so that you get* [a benefit removing your pain], *right?"* In that case, the other salesperson would be putting your prospect on the spot to say, *"Well, no."* And the salesperson would have been directly questioning the performance or the offering of the competition. By putting the question instead in the PICTURE PERFECT format, you eliminated both of these potential causes of uneasiness. You avoided attacking your competition, and you made it much easier for your prospect to face his or her problem. All you did was present the ideal situation to your prospect. He or she does not have to say to you, *"I have a problem."* Your prospect can merely point out that the service he or she currently receives, or would receive from your other competitors who have talked to the prospect, does not meet the high standard you have cited. That is one of the reasons you can beat traditional selling using The Wedge.

When using PICTURE PERFECT, you can build the momentum you need to eliminate your competition and to get the current provider fired if there is one by using the "shelf" technique. You ask one PICTURE PERFECT question, let your prospect respond, and then reply, *"May we put that on the shelf for a moment?"* This lets your prospect know that you will deal with it shortly. Then you ask another PICTURE PERFECT question, and do the same thing. After you have, say, three or four PICTURE PERFECT questions on the shelf, you have set the stage for a gestalt moment in which your prospect will be thinking and feeling something like, *"Gee. I've got some things to deal with."* So you take the issues off the shelf and move forward from there, with your prospect more emotionally committed than he or she would have been if you were dealing with only one issue.

Two Kinds of Preliminary Questions

In the real world, of course, you cannot walk into your prospects' offices and immediately start asking them PICTURE PERFECT questions. It would be unnatural, and it would be seen by your prospects as manipulative. So you have to lay the groundwork with a few preliminary questions. There are two ways you will be doing this.

First, you will go right after any active pain that your prospect might have at the forefront of his or her mind by asking "fishnet" questions. Fishnet questions are general questions such as, *"How's business?"* and *"Any problems lately that you'd like to discuss?"* Sometimes, your prospect will bite early. He or she will bring up a specific pain. When that happens, you can use the Reactive Wedge, a question in response to an active pain that your prospect has volunteered. It is the reactive version of PICTURE PERFECT, and it goes like this:

> *"I'm curious. When you tried to* [remove the pain] *by using* [a remedy or benefit], *how did that go?"*

In your reactive question, you have succeeded in focusing your prospect on the gap between ideal PICTURE PERFECT service and the service currently being provided. Plus, you did not attack your competition. Your question assumed that your competition could or would fix the problem, or already had fixed it if there were a provider already handling the account.

Next, you will ask your prospect "qualifying" questions. Qualifying questions help you determine whether the conditions exist for you to ask a PICTURE PERFECT question. A qualifying question might be, *"Do you deal with* [broad subject area]*?"* or *"Have you had any* [events related to broad subject area] *lately?"* If your prospect says yes, then you can ask the PICTURE PERFECT question. You can think of the PICTURE PERFECT question in this sense as a Proactive Wedge. Unlike the Reactive Wedge, which is designed to respond to a pain volunteered by the prospect from his or her active memory, the Proactive Wedge is intended to activate a latent pain and bring it into your prospect's active memory. A Proactive Wedge is a PICTURE PERFECT question:

> *"I'm curious. When you receive* [a specific service] *so that you don't have to worry about* [a specific pain], *are you comfortable with that process?"*

When you are looking for pain, you are making an educated guess based on your precall research about what the prospect's concerns are likely to be. The proactive PICTURE PERFECT question is straightforward. As you talk to your prospect, you can keep asking PICTURE PERFECT questions. Some will miss, and some will hit. When they miss, you can move on. When they hit, you have something to work with.

Compared with traditional selling, The Wedge will engage you in a more effective dialogue with your prospect

93

that will give you a considerably greater chance to win the account. You are helping your prospect discover pain that he or she may have forgotten. You are initiating a process to get your competition fired or dismissed from consideration without saying anything bad about them.

Thinking Visually

The power of PICTURE PERFECT lies not in the idea of perfection but in the picture of that perfection. *Picture* is the key word. Your prospects must be able to visualize what perfect service looks like. They must have a clear, specific image in their minds. To give them this picture, you will need to use concrete, specific words—staying low on the ladder of abstraction. Always be asking yourself, *"Is there a way I can make this more concrete?"*

The example of the ideal service, not the fact that your service is ideal, is the most powerful way of differentiating yourself from your competition. Remember, too, what we said earlier: It is not just *what* you do but *how* you do it. Explaining how you do things takes you down the ladder of abstraction to the level of concrete detail where you can differentiate yourself from the competition in a way that has a much greater impact on your prospect. Why? Because you are getting your prospect to think visually. What they truly understand they can appreciate.

What Visuals Do You Use?

Think about the ways your company provides service—the specific things you do on a day-to-day basis. How do you go about getting the job done? What are the tasks your people complete, the actual way they do something as opposed to merely what it is that they do? This is where you will find the concrete differences that make you superior to your competition.

To prepare yourself to win more new business rather than settle for opportunities to present, one of the best investments of your time that you can make is in talking to people at your company about how they do their jobs. This is where you will find the tangible, specific things that make you better and different—the way a bank does a cash flow analysis for a business, a helpful customer usage report from a water company, a tax reduction checklist provided by a CPA, an exposure analysis by an insurance agency, a no-wait rental car service, and so on. These are the kinds of things that will enable you to drive The Wedge. As we discussed in Chapter 2, your business probably has 12 to 18 specific examples of your service strengths that can be matched up favorably against your competition's service weaknesses, and that can be presented as concrete, visual examples.

Like most salespeople, you may be a little uncomfortable with taking time off the circuit and working at your office conferring with your own people. You would rather be out there presenting to more prospects, driving that bus with an explosive device that will detonate if you slow down. Time is money, you remind yourself. For every moment that you are not in front of a prospect, you might have lost an opportunity. But stop and consider your role. If all you do is go into sales calls without a particular strategy for each individual prospect, you are no more useful than an advertisement your company could place or a sales brochure it could distribute. In fact, however, you are more than a marketing tool—you are a sales *person*. Each sales call is a unique encounter, not a one-size-fits-all opportunity. The Wedge may require you to adjust your instincts. But the payoff is worth it—fewer sales calls to win more new business.

Unfortunately, many sales managers reinforce the notion that time spent by sales representatives at the office is not as productive as outside time. These managers have not been trained to show their reps the value of interviewing their colleagues, drilling down and coming up with the gems that will help them win more accounts. As we discuss in Part III of this book, the sales manager who makes this gem-finding process an integral part of the regular sales meeting can significantly boost the success of the sales team.

Built-In Tension

PICTURE PERFECT also works because in every prospect-provider relationship there are potential weak points for you to identify and exploit. It is only natural that clients want more, and providers want to keep their clients happy while doing less. That is not to say that clients are greedy and providers are lazy. It's human nature.

If I'm your seller or provider, I want to do the least I can to keep you happy. I do want to keep you happy, to be sure, but I want to do it as efficiently as I can, so that I can increase my income by having more time to handle other accounts. If I'm your buyer, on the other hand, I want the most I can get from you. I want you to make me a priority customer. Your other accounts are not a concern of mine.

This service-related tension gives salespeople an opening to drive The Wedge between the prospect and the provider by offering a PICTURE PERFECT example of an *ideal* level of service as opposed to the *necessary* level of service that the current provider is delivering.

Will PICTURE PERFECT Work Every Time?

As a reliable pain detector, the PICTURE PERFECT question has an excellent track record. I cannot guarantee it will work every time, but I can tell you it has a high probability of success. Generally, there are five things that you might encounter that could cause it not to work: (1) you did not establish a rapport with your prospect at the start of your sales call; (2) your precall strategic research fell short and you did not find out that your competition was already performing or offering the ideal service you described; (3) you were too vague in the way you put the PICTURE PERFECT question; (4) you did not mention the pain to be avoided; or (5) what you brought up was not relevant to your prospect.

With practice, you should get better and better at the PICTURE PERFECT technique. Remember: The more specific and concrete the example, the more powerful your PICTURE PERFECT question will be. This can be a trying exercise, but I can tell you from experience that it is where money is made.

The Conversation

As we go through the six steps of The Wedge Sales Call from PICTURE PERFECT through REHEARSAL, I will be giving you six simple conversational phrases that you can use as you go from one step to the other. With a little practice, you can internalize the Wedge technique without having to stop and think about each step.

Here is the key phrase we have learned for the PICTURE PERFECT step:

"I'm curious. When you receive [a specific service] *so that you don't have to worry about* [a specific pain], *are you comfortable with that process?"*

Try it out. Think about examples that apply to your own company. Repeat each one, using the sentence above to set it up. The more you do it, the more natural it will become.

If you are a financial planner, for example, you might say:

"I'm curious. When you see all your holdings listed on one consolidated sheet—your mutual funds, 401(k), brokerage account, checking account, real estate investments, life insurance, your spouse's IRA, and so on—so that you don't have to wonder what each one is doing to advance your overall allocation strategy, are you comfortable with that process?"

Or if you are a banker you might say:

"I'm curious. When your banker came out six months after your credit was renewed to do a business plan review, and he

got out your business plan to talk about your new locations, products, employees, and cash flow needs so that you could develop a plan to finance your growth and you wouldn't have to worry about getting stuck with a marginal line of credit, were you comfortable with how he did that?"

If you would like an example that applies specifically to your type of business, you can visit my company's web site at www.thewedge.net and consult our list or request additional information.

Step 2: Take Away

By creating a PICTURE PERFECT, you have helped your prospect visualize an example of the ideal service that he or she is not receiving. You have found the pain, and prompted your prospect to bring that pain into his or her active consciousness. The question now is the degree of that pain. How much does it matter to your prospect? Is it significant, or just a minor irritant that is not important to him or her? Is it powerful enough to motivate your prospect to make a change and hire you?

The technique for measuring your prospect's pain is the TAKE AWAY. A well-known selling tactic, the TAKE AWAY is designed to see if your prospect cares about something enough to object when it is taken off the table. In your case, you will use the TAKE AWAY to see if the PICTURE PERFECT matters enough to the prospect that he or she will protest when you appear to be downplaying its importance. The key phrase for the TAKE AWAY is this:

> *"Well, perhaps it's not that important because* [insert a reason here]. *"*

For example, suppose you are an IT salesperson offering a company a systems management server. You know from your precall research that your competition, whether it is the current IT vendor or someone else seeking the account, does not provide security capabilities as comprehensive as yours. During your sales call, you ask a PICTURE PERFECT question:

> *"I'm curious. When your server was set up to automatically install patches, hot fixes, and other software updates on all of your desktops so that you don't have to worry about viruses getting into your system and people using outdated applications, were you comfortable with that process?"*

Your prospect then replies, *"Well, we don't quite do it that way, but we know whenever we need to install something important."*

A salesperson relying on traditional selling might at this moment blurt out, *"It's not done for you automatically?"*

Instead, you are going to calmly reply,

> *"Well, perhaps it's not that important because your internal IT person can always send an e-mail alerting everybody to download and install the necessary update."*

By minimizing your prospect's pain and taking away the service and benefit he would have gotten from the PIC-TURE PERFECT, you are inviting the prospect to speak up before you move on. If the prospect agrees with you that it is not that important, you might as well move on. On the other hand, if the response is, *"No. It does matter because . . . ,"* then you have confirmed that you have a specific pain that you can use to keep driving The Wedge—and you have done a favor for your prospect by making him see what he will lose if he does not take action.

Notice, too, how the TAKE AWAY statement says, *"Perhaps it's not that important,"* rather than *"Perhaps it's not that important to you."* By omitting two words—"to you"—you avoid putting your prospect on the defensive.

If you do not have a plausible reason to suggest why it is not a big deal, you can still use the TAKE AWAY by merely saying, *"Perhaps it's not that important."* The principle is the same.

Self-Discovery

The Wedge strategy is about helping your prospects discover what they really want, as opposed to pushing them in a predetermined direction. From your precall research and your knowledge of the industry you service, you already have an understanding of the kinds of issues likely to be of concern to prospects. As you test your prospect's pain by creating various PICTURE PERFECT images, you can measure each instance of pain by using the TAKE AWAY. The TAKE AWAY itself is a simple procedure. You state the cost of inaction, and then you dismiss it.

Using a traditional sales approach, you might upon discovering your prospect's pain try to hammer the point home. You might say, *"No worry there. We make it a point to provide* [the specific service]. *If you were our client, this would never happen. Would you like to get started with us?"*

Feeling pressure, your prospect might well respond, *"I appreciate what you're saying. It's a concern for us, but let me think about it some more."* Psychologically, you have caused your prospect to take a step back.

The Wedge approach, on the other hand, leaves it to the prospect to tell you how important the issue is. Using the TAKE AWAY, you say to the prospect, *"Perhaps it's not that important because* [insert a reason]."

If it does matter to your prospect, he will object to your TAKE AWAY. In this case, your prospect is asserting his need rather than having you define what that need is. You have allowed your prospect to stay in control of the situation and, indeed, you have encouraged him to begin telling you what he would like. Rather than pushing your prospect away, you have used the TAKE AWAY to prompt him to push back—but to push back in your favor.

Wanting What's *Not* Yours, Not Wanting What *Is*

The TAKE AWAY works because of a phenomenon in negotiations pointed out by author and lecturer Robert J. Ringer. According to Ringer, negotiations are like the "dating game." Each party wants what he or she *cannot* have, and does not want what he or she *can* have. It is similar to a boy or girl in high school who plays hard to get. The boy/girl theory helps explain the power of the TAKE AWAY. Suddenly, the prospect might lose the PICTURE PERFECT benefit after all, so he or she speaks up lest it get away.

The Attitude of the TAKE AWAY

As simple as it appears to be, the TAKE AWAY is difficult for many salespeople to master. In my years of sales training, I have seen otherwise skilled professionals struggle with how to do it naturally and smoothly. The major reason for this is that when you do a TAKE AWAY you are being unnatural, saying the opposite of what you mean. You are stating the reverse of what you truly would like to say. You are calmly suggesting to your prospect, *"Perhaps it's not that important because . . . ,"* but you are screaming inside, *"Are you nuts? You have to deal with this!"*

Again, your strategy is to let your prospect feel comfortably in control of the conversation. If you were to hammer home the benefit of the PICTURE PERFECT example and simply try to get your prospect to agree with you, you would be selling and your prospect would start to back off. Instead, you are letting your prospect think about the benefit on his or her own, and come to a conclusion without pressure.

Because the TAKE AWAY sends an incongruous, contradictory message, you will get your prospect's attention when you use it. During the moment that he or she looks at you a little quizzically, one of two things will happen. Either your prospect will be thinking, *"Wait. I do need this."* Or else he or she will be thinking, *"Maybe it isn't that important."*

Your attitude as you do the TAKE AWAY can have a major effect on how well you execute it. I tell most of my clients to go into the TAKE AWAY step thinking of this statement that I once heard: "I am independently wealthy. I don't need the money because the degree to which I need your money is the degree that I'm subject to your manipulation." This frame of mind should enable you to appear as cool as a cucumber while you oddly downplay what you just brought up a moment before as important.

The attitude of the TAKE AWAY is a good attitude for selling in general, for strengthening your ability to help your prospects discover and meet their true needs instead of letting them kick you around and get you off track. Would Warren Buffett, Bill Gates, Ross Perot, or Donald Trump put up with the stuff that most salespeople tolerate? Of course not. And neither should you. If you're going to truly help your prospects, you need to be strong and confident and resist any attempt they make to play games and manipulate you.

Your Professional Responsibility

By using the TAKE AWAY, you help your prospects make the right decision for themselves. That brings us to another reason that some salespeople have trouble doing the TAKE AWAY. They do not want the added responsibility of going the extra mile to make a real difference in people's lives. They would rather focus their sales call on getting from point A to point B with some positive outcome, whether or not it addresses the prospect's most important needs.

For salespeople who claim to believe in the services

and products they sell and the companies they represent, The Wedge puts their claim to the test. If what you are telling your prospects is true, then you have a duty to help them discover how they can benefit from what you offer, and why they should act now, in their own interest, to take advantage of it. By failing to win the business, you are not only letting yourself and your company down; you are letting your prospect down. A number of salespeople I have worked with have come to that realization. Many of them have told me, "If I see real problems facing my prospect, and if I can't find a way to get the prospect to see that, then it's my fault."

I know this firsthand. My late father worked hard, as did my mother, in raising my brothers and me near Lubbock, Texas. My dad knew that if he ever perished, God forbid, Social Security would not be enough for my mother to live on. He bought only a small life insurance policy, though, in order to save on the monthly premiums. As a result, my mother was not adequately provided for when my father passed away. How great it would have been if a good life insurance agent had cared enough to sell my father what my parents really needed. This is a good lesson for all of us as salespeople. If we can't get our prospects to understand and see what they really need, and motivate them to act, then we have let them down.

The Conversation

Let us review where we are in The Wedge Sales Call. You established a rapport with your prospect. You then began asking the right questions to find your prospect's pain. That set up The Wedge, and here are the two key phrases you used to move into each step:

PICTURE PERFECT: *"I'm curious. When you receive* [a specific service] *so that you don't have to worry about* [a specific pain], *are you comfortable with that process?"*

TAKE AWAY: *"Well, perhaps it's not that important because* [insert a reason]."

By using examples of PICTURE PERFECT to get your prospects to focus on their pain, and by employing the TAKE AWAY to determine whether each pain is important enough to your prospects to motivate them to consider hiring you and firing the current provider or ruling out your other competitors, you have finished the Problem Phase. Next, I show you how to help your prospect come up with the solution that he or she truly wants in order to remedy the pain that you have activated.

CHAPTER 5

Proposing a Remedy— The Solution Phase

U p until now, you have focused on creating rapport with your prospect, finding his or her pain, and measuring the intensity of that pain. Now it is time to help your prospect describe the solution he or she truly wants. That is another key strength and difference of The Wedge as opposed to traditional selling. You are not going to offer your prospect a solution and ask him or her to accept it. Instead, you are going to help your prospect propose the solution, and get your prospect to decide what to do to make it happen.

Step 3: Vision Box

It should come as no surprise that prospects, like many salespeople, have trouble expressing *exactly* what they want. Prospects also define what they want with terms such as "competitive prices" and "consistent quality." In their own business, they, too, are "dedicated to excellence" and have "strategies for growth." Your challenge will be to help your prospects move down the ladder of abstraction and describe the details of their vision.

A vision is an endless sort of thing. It suggests peering into the heavens and contemplating perfection. During the VISION BOX step, you are going to educe from your prospects the details that give reality to their vision, drawing out of them the specific, concrete things that they really want to happen.

Let me ask you this: If you leave a sales call without knowing exactly what your prospect wants—the what, how, who, when, where, and why of it—can you deliver it to the prospect? Of course you can't. And if the prospect doesn't spell it out for you, can you develop a proposal that gives them what they want? Obviously not. You would come away from that sales call with neither of you certain about the particulars. It happens more than it should. The salesperson returns to the prospect after the initial meeting, bringing along a proposal based on guesses and assumptions. The two of them go through the prospect's objections and make changes, and the selling process gets prolonged much more than it needs to be.

The VISION BOX step will enable you to shorten the time it takes for you and your prospect to get in sync on the solution. You are going to help your prospects take their vision, and then box that vision as a deliverable. What is in the box? It contains a precise description of people, places, and things from the real world—physical objects and specific actions, a picture in sharp focus that your prospect can visualize rather than merely generally grasp as a concept. It has no abstractions. It consists of deliverables.

Imagine a couple asking a travel agent to plan their ideal vacation for them. They may see themselves on a warm, sandy beach in the Virgin Islands, located near recreational facilities to enjoy while they are there. But as soon as the agent starts planning for their vision, all sorts of details arise. What are the dates? What about plane reservations? What kind of lodging do they want? How will they get around while they are there?

When I'm conducting workshops, I often ask my audience to divide up into pairs and plan each partner's ideal vacation. I tell them to ask all the questions they can think of so that they can book a trip for their partner with no more questions. It usually takes about 15 minutes for them to accomplish their task. One day, however, one of my workshop participants was done in 60 seconds.

"How did you finish so quickly?" I asked him.

"It was easy," he said. "My partner simply wanted to go to a beach in Florida."

If you look at a map of Florida, you will notice that there are nearly 1,200 miles of coastline starting in the west at Pensacola, dipping south past Tampa and Fort Myers, down into the Keys, and from there up to Miami and north back up the Atlantic coast to Jacksonville. You may have an ideal vision of a beach in Florida, but if that is the only thing you ask for without specifying anything further, you could wind up surrounded by a marsh or sharing your space with alligators.

So you will begin the VISION BOX step with our next conversational phrase:

> *"In regard to* [area of concern], *what would you like to see happen?"*

Even after you have put it this way, your prospect will almost always respond at first with something vague and undefined. From this starting point, you will need to follow up with specific questions that prompt the prospect to home in on precisely what he or she is trying to change. Your prospects at this point will know they are dissatisfied.

They may think about such things as "faster service" or "more technical support," but those goals mean nothing until the specific outcomes they represent are pinned down in concrete language.

To get your prospect to fill in the box and define the solution he or she wants, you can ask these six questions:

1. *What?*

   What would you like to have happen? What is the practical result you want in concrete terms?

2. *How?*

   How should the result be achieved? What does the process look like? What are the means it will take?

3. *Who?*

   Whom do you see involved from your company? Who else? What will their roles be?

4. *When?*

   When do you want it? Immediately? Ninety days from now? What will happen at what point?

5. *Where?*

   Where will it be handled? At your service center? Corporate headquarters? Branch offices?

6. *Why?*

   Why is it important? What makes it a priority? Why do you value it?

Your task in asking these questions is to elicit concrete language and images from your prospect that describe precisely what he or she expects to happen. Without such a graphic depiction, you will not know for certain what your prospect wants from you. Educated guesses are no substitute. Some salespeople and their prospects too easily fall into the trap of wishful thinking. They start to feel a bond, they begin nodding in agreement with each other, and soon they find themselves talking each other into doing business without filling in the details. As then President Ronald Reagan said after one of his summit meetings with then Soviet President Mikhail Gorbachev, "Trust, but verify." Or, to quote another short and wise motto: Never assume.

The VISION BOX is a much more powerful offer than the boilerplate in your company's shell proposals. By educing what the prospects want, you have gotten them to convey in their own terms how they want to be served. The proposal that results will be what they expect, not a first draft that sidetracks you into having to overcome objections.

For example, imagine you are a wholesaler talking to an appliance retailer whose current supplier has been inconsistent in the timely delivery of dryers that, as a result, dwindle and go out of stock. You ask your prospect, *"In regard to dryer delivery, what would you like to see happen?"* And your prospect replies, *"I want dryers in our stores when we need them."*

No doubt your competition promised your prospect that very result. If you left the discussion there, you would be making the same promise. If you did that, you would be offering nothing new. You would have nothing to sell. So you are going to use the questions of the VISION BOX to drill down and get your prospect to describe the better process that will get better results:

Seller: "**What** would you like to have happen?"

Prospect: "We want no more than a five-day turnaround from the day we place an order."

Seller: "Order what exactly?"

Prospect: "Blazing Heat and Desert Air dryers have been the problem."

Seller: "**How** would you like them shipped?"

Prospect: "By using the least expensive shipping with a five-day guarantee."

Seller: "**Who** will be involved from your company?"

Prospect: "Each store manager will notify our buyer, who will contact the wholesaler."

Seller: "**When** would you like to set all this up?"

Prospect: "Within the next 30 days."

Seller: "**Where** will it be handled in your company's organization?"

Prospect: "Each store manager will be responsible for reporting low inventory?"

Seller: "**What** do you mean by 'low'?"

Prospect: "When we have no more than a dozen Blazing Heat dryers or two dozen Desert Air dryers in stock."

Seller: "**Why** again is this so critical among all your inventory needs?"

Prospect: "We don't want to lose any more customers over this, and those two brands have been the problem."

At times, your prospects may tell you that they do not really know what they want. It may be tough to get them to start talking. When this happens, a third-party story can be helpful. Describe for them a similar situation where a prospect had trouble drilling down into the details, and how by your asking questions the prospect's specific needs came into focus. But be sure to relate it to your prospect and what he or she wants, not merely to recite it as a third-party story. Your conversation might go something like this:

> *Seller:* "So in regard to what we discussed, what would you like to see happen?"
>
> *Prospect:* "I don't know."
>
> *Seller:* "That's not unusual. I had a client in a similar situation to yours. His retail outlet sold home theater equipment. So I started asking him questions about his operation to get him going. This helped him focus, so he could get into the details of what he wanted. I'd ask him what he wanted to happen, who would need to do what, and so on. Does this make sense for you as a way we can get into this?"

If you had merely told your prospect the story and talked about yourself, he or she would have started to tune out and shut down. Instead, you related it to your prospect, and kept the focus on his or her situation.

Finally, after your prospects have defined the deliverables that go in the VISION BOX, it is a good idea to ask one last time before moving on, *"Anything else?"* This prompts your prospects to think back over what they have just told you. Often, they will come up with an important point skipped over.

There is another reason to get your prospect to be as clear-cut as possible. In most businesses and industries, you can predict with reasonable accuracy that your rivals offer the same kinds of services and products you do. They just have not made the extra effort to find out which ones matter most to your prospect. If your competition had done so, you would have discovered less pain. As a result, driving The Wedge would have been considerably more difficult if not essentially impossible.

Now you have a clear vision of what your prospect wants. You have almost completed the Solution Phase, but there is one more step.

Step 4: Replay

The REPLAY is your repeating back to the prospect what you understand it is that he or she wants. To do this, you will use our next conversational snippet:

> *"Here's what I'm hearing you say you want.* [Repeat what the prospect said] *Have I got that right?"*

As applied to our example, you will say to the retailer:

> *"Here's what I'm hearing you say you want. You want guaranteed five-day turnaround on Blazing Heat and Desert Air dryers with the least expensive shipping. Each of your store managers would be responsible for notifying your buyer of low inventory when you're down to 12 Blazing Heat or 24 Desert Air dryers, and your buyer would contact the wholesaler and order a dozen of either or both that become low. You'd like to fix this within the next 30 days and not have any more customers who can't get what they expect when they visit one of your stores. Have I got that right?"*

115

This may seem simplistic, even superfluous. But there are three strategic reasons for the REPLAY.

First, notice how you told the prospect you were hearing what *"you say you want."* By using the pronoun *you*, you are confirming that the VISION BOX is the prospect's solution. Also notice that you used the word *want*. When people want something, they will take action to get it. If they are merely interested, they will defer action or not act at all.

Second, by using the REPLAY, you are sending your prospect an important signal that you know how to listen. You understand your prospect's concern, and you are speaking in his or her language to address it. This helps solidify the bond of comfort, credibility, and trust that you have begun building with your prospect.

Third, remember how the TAKE AWAY helped to reinforce the prospect's desire for the PICTURE PERFECT? The REPLAY works in the same way to reinforce the VISION BOX, and it shifts the dialogue in your favor. When you play back to prospects what they have just told you they want, you are positioning yourself as the person to provide it. This is a subtle but important transition. You have begun to establish yourself in the prospect's mind as the person who can deliver the solution. Yet, you have not once offered to handle the account. Using The Wedge rather than traditional selling, you have confidently laid the groundwork for your prospect to do the right thing.

During the VISION BOX and the REPLAY, you may be tempted to talk about what *you* can do for your prospect. When you know your capabilities, and when you hear your prospect spelling out a need that you can meet and then some, your inclination may be to jump right in and start touting all your strengths. We all remember the kid in our fourth-grade class who always knew the answer to a question the teacher had just asked, the one who frantically waved his hand and said, "Pick me. Pick me."

Whatever you do during the Solution Phase, it is important to stay away from the words *I* and *me*. If you lapse into promoting yourself and your company at this critical juncture, your prospect will take a step backward psychologically from making a commitment. Prospects begin to talk less when they feel the pressure of a salesperson's self-promotion. If you start speaking in the first person, it will create a moment of discomfort, and your prospect will begin to feel as if he or she is losing control of the conversation.

As I mentioned earlier, it is helpful to think of your prospect as a personal friend, rather than as the other party in a buyer-seller relationship. Imagine, for example, that a friend of yours wants to have a swimming pool put in his backyard, and you happen to be in the business. Because you and he are friends, you share his excitement over his plans. However, you are not going to make a presentation to him of your services. Instead, you and he start talking about his vision for the pool. He wants a kidney-shaped, heated concrete pool with a diving board at the deep end. You start asking him questions to bring his vision into clearer focus. Everything is going fine, and you are enjoying a relaxing exchange of ideas and suggestions. What if you were to blurt out, "Pete, I'd love to build this pool for you. Can I give you an estimate?" At that moment, you and Pete would stop conversing freely. You and he would become a seller and buyer in a negotiation. Pete would stop telling you what he really wants. He would start talking about what he can afford. Your conversation would get more stilted, and you and he would no longer be talking excitedly about his dream.

The Wedge Sales Call is designed to create an atmosphere in which your prospect can talk to you as if he or she were talking to a friend. Not once have you asked for the business. Your focus has been on listening, and subtly guiding your prospect from step to step in his or her process of self-discovery. When your prospects see you as the person who can take them from where they are to where they want to be, they will ask you in—and when you are being asked, you have all the power.

The Conversation

You and your prospect have used the VISION BOX and the REPLAY to agree on exactly what he or she wants. Here are the four key phrases you have used so far on your way to winning the business:

PICTURE PERFECT: *"I'm curious. When you receive* [a specific service] *so that you don't have to worry about* [a specific pain], *are you comfortable with that process?"*

TAKE AWAY: *"Well, perhaps it's not that important because* [insert a reason]."

VISION BOX: *"In regard to* [area of concern], *what would you like to see happen?"*

118

REPLAY: *"Here's what I'm hearing you say you want.* [Repeat what the prospect said.] *Have I got that right?"*

By getting your prospects to clearly and concretely describe what they want, by helping them identify the deliverables that go in the VISION BOX, and by giving them a REPLAY to confirm that you and they share the same, specific image of the remedy to their pain, you have effectively completed the Solution Phase.

The next chapter shows you how to get your prospects to invite you to do business with them. Instead of pushing them to shake hands and call it a deal, you are going to encourage *them* to take the initiative. And when they do, you are going to step into the space you have created by driving The Wedge between your prospects and your competition. You are going to take the final step to get your competition fired—either from the account or from consideration for it—without saying anything bad about them.

6

Getting Your Competition Fired— The Commitment Phase

Throughout The Wedge Sales Call, your approach has been to help your prospect feel in control of the pace and the content of the meeting. You have been a tour guide, taking your prospect along a path of self-discovery. Once you initially got your prospect comfortable and began asking a few questions, you deliberately pulled back and let your prospect do most of the talking.

In the Commitment Phase, you keep doing the same thing as you move toward closing. Unlike traditional selling, The Wedge is not about asking your prospects for an agreement to do business. The Wedge strategy is about getting them to invite you in, getting them to make the decision.

Some people mistake this apparently laissez-faire approach to selling as too uncertain and soft. They say a great communicator with excellent closing skills should take advantage of those skills and get the prospect to sign up before the magic moment passes. Moreover, shouldn't a salesperson show that he or she cares enough to ask for the prospect's business? Those who have mastered The Wedge know better. They know that the strongest position to be in is for the prospect to invite you in. That is where you get the leverage you need to overcome the number one obstacle to winning the deal—getting your competition fired. If your prospects cannot fire your competition, they cannot hire you. So the key is to get your prospects to invite you in, to confirm that they have the authority and willingness to fire your competitor, and then to help them do just that.

When I was a young boy in the 1960s, my buddies

and I used to hang around in the yard outside a friend's house. On some days, his mother would come to the door and invite us all inside to have Kool-Aid and cookies. When that happened, we would charge right in, grab the cookies and pour the Kool-Aid, and make ourselves at home. Now and then, though, his mother would stick her head outside and shout, "Son! You get in here right now!" So the rest of us would wait awhile, and then we would walk up to the door cautiously. We'd ask, "May we come in?" And, if we did get inside, it was a whole different ball game. One of us would ask tentatively, "Could we have something to drink?" This is an example of how getting invited in gives you much greater leverage to go after what you really want. And in a selling situation, it fosters the relationship you need with your prospect in order to deal directly with the issue of the incumbent.

Step 5: White Flag

To get yourself invited in, you are going to avoid the traditional role of the salesperson who is expected to pop the question with a trial close. Instead, you are going to wave a WHITE FLAG. You are going to figuratively throw up your arms, look at your prospect, and simply say:

"So, what would you like me to do?"

If you have done a reasonably astute job of driving The Wedge, your prospect's reaction should be immediate and positive. He or she may not literally say, *"Could you*

123

start working for us next Tuesday?" However, your prospect will likely say something affirmative along the lines of *"Well, would you like to put together a proposal for us?"*

Because you just got invited in, you now have the leverage you need to move ahead and deal with the incumbent. What helped you get invited in was that you in no way pressured your prospect to accept anything in particular. By waving the WHITE FLAG, you left it up to the prospect to make the call in his or her own way.

Step 6: Rehearsal

So your prospect has invited you in. That's great. You waved the WHITE FLAG, and you got in. Your prospect asked you to go ahead and prepare a proposal. Now you have two options. You can either walk away happily and return in a few days with a proposal, or you can put the proposal aside for a moment and use the opportunity to deal with the incumbent.

If you choose the first option, you could thank your prospect for his or her confidence, and promise to get back in a few days with specific plans for dealing with the concerns you were asked to address. You could walk away believing that you have a deal in the bank once you dot all the i's and cross all the t's. A few days later, you could call or stop by with your proposal. Your prospect would graciously thank you for it, and thank you again for your time. Your prospect would tell you how much he or she appreciated your thoughtfulness and responsiveness. Then your prospect would stress how much he or she looks forward to doing business with you at some point in the future. And finally, your prospect would extend you the courtesy of inviting you to call from time to time to see if that point is approaching. You know, of course, what would have happened. Your prospect would have used the interlude after your sales call to check in with the current provider, asking questions about service. Not being anyone's fool and knowing that something was going on, the provider would have leaped into action. After some reminiscing and hand-holding with your prospect, the provider would have agreed to meet or exceed everything that you said you would do. You would have just gotten rolled.

So here's the other option. Step 6 of The Wedge Sales Call, the REHEARSAL, is designed to protect you from getting rolled. How? That brings us to our next conversational phrase. When your prospect asks for a proposal, here is what you say:

"That's the easy part. May we talk about the hard part?"

And your prospect will ask, *"The hard part? What do you mean?"* So you will explain.

You: "Suppose in a few days I'm back with the proposal. It has everything you said you want. The pricing is competitive. And you've checked us out and you know we're for real, that we do what we say we'll do. What happens then?"

Prospect: "I'd say we have a new rep."

You: "Well, that creates a dilemma. Can we talk about it?"

Prospect: "Sure."

You: "The problem is that when you decide that we're your new rep, how will you tell your other rep that it's over?"

Prospect: "I'll just tell them. It's business."

You: "And you're saying it's that easy? You'll just tell them they're gone?"

Prospect: "Well, I'll cross that bridge when we come to it."

You: "You say that. Can I tell you what's going to happen?"

Prospect: "What?"

You: "Here's what will happen. Your rep will find out you want to make a change. He'll want to come see you. When he gets here, he'll talk about all he's done for you, and how great your relationship is. He'll tell you that if it's price, he can match it. If it's product, his is just as good. And he'll tell you he can provide at least the same service everyone else can. When he does all this, how will you handle it?"

Now you are at the moment of truth. You are about to find out whether you are going to get the account, whether your prospect is going to fire your competition.

Firing someone is seldom an easy decision, as you know if you have ever been in this position. You might have employed someone who was just not working out. You realize you need to let the person go, but he or she is a nice individual, and has a family to help support. So you start to get cold feet. You may fear the disruption it could cause or begin to feel guilty about not doing more to make things work, or out of loyalty you are just too reluctant to pull the trigger.

The chances are pretty good that the person who already has the account, your competition, will want to come see your prospect. Once there, your competitor will try to make your prospect feel guilty, or create fear of change, or leverage the loyalty button. If you have not rehearsed your prospect on how to deal with this when the time comes, the chances are good that your prospect will get hooked. And when that happens, you lose.

This is the importance of the REHEARSAL technique. If your prospect can't rehearse in front of you, how will he or she be able to tell your competition directly that it's over? How will your prospect resist getting hooked by guilt, fear, or loyalty when the current provider stops by in person with wine and cheese?

The REHEARSAL also helps your prospect prepare emotionally for firing your competition. It is a way of allowing your prospect to let off steam in order to deal with the moment in a calmer, more controlled fashion when it arrives.

The REHEARSAL is the true close for you. It is where you establish with no uncertainty whether your prospect has both the authority and the determination to fire or dismiss your competitors and hire you. The REHEARSAL is where you get the *commitment* that you can provide the *solution* to the *problem*, the culmination of all three phases and all six steps of The Wedge Sales Call.

As a general rule, I would recommend asking just enough questions to satisfy yourself that your prospect has the determination to do the deed. You will be relying on your intuitive judgment to an extent, but at some point you will be fairly certain your prospect is ready to act.

When that moment arrives, it is time for you to acknowledge your prospect's close:

"Are you comfortable with everything? [Prospect responds affirmatively.] *So it's done. Great. I'll get to work."*

By asking your prospects if they are comfortable, you are making sure they have gone through the emotional preview of the firing and are at peace with themselves about doing it. When they answer yes, you then make it official by declaring, *"So it's done."*

Notice your inflection. You say, *"So it's done."* You do not ask, *"So it's done?"* You assume the deal, celebrate with the word *"Great,"* and begin taking over the account with the words *"I'll get to work."*

Will The Wedge work every time? Of course not. There will be meetings where in the first few minutes you know from experience that you are not going to get the business. And there are some outstanding prospect-provider relationships out there that not even a sledge, let alone a wedge, could crack. But The Wedge works most of the time. If you have uncovered your competitive advantage and developed your proactive services, if you have done your precall strategy research and found the most powerful way to communicate that competitive advantage, if during your sales call you have found out what your prospect truly wants and have gotten yourself invited in, and if you have rehearsed your prospect on firing your competition, then most of the time you will be able to win the business.

Since its initial formulation a decade ago, The Wedge strategy has helped thousands of sales professionals and hundreds of companies, including some of America's very largest, achieve some pretty remarkable results. It has worked for small businesses with 20 or 30 employees as well as for major corporations with thousands of employees.

You would think a large company with a major brand name would have its selling process down, that it would know the most effective way to win business. In reality, I've found in working with some of these multibillion dollar organizations that, if they had to appear before Judge Judy tomorrow morning and state what makes them different and better, most of the time they couldn't say. Why? Because they have not drilled down and identified their true competitive advantage. They are not selling their proactive services platform, the most powerful differentiation they have in today's marketplace.

The Wedge works because—to repeat our mantra—it disciplines sellers to proactively control the experiences of their clients, making their future more predictable. It is not your company's price, product, or reactive service that gives you the greatest advantage in most competitive services industries. It is your proactive service. This is what gives you the leverage you need to get your competition fired.

Recap

So you have taken your prospect through the six steps of The Wedge Sales Call. From the moment you walked in and commented on the skiing photograph to when your prospect assured you that he or she was ready to give your competition the bad news, you helped your prospect come to the right decision:

- You created a rapport with the prospect by putting him or her at ease. You told your prospect a story about a similar client whose problem you fixed. You passed the comfort and credibility tests.

- You asked preliminary questions to begin your search for pain.

- You created a PICTURE PERFECT of ideal service, one that deliberately reflected a strength of yours in contrast to a weakness of your competition, and one that prompted your prospect to feel the pain of being underserved, giving you something to sell.

- You used the TAKE AWAY to measure your prospect's pain, triggering your prospect to insist on the benefit of the PICTURE PERFECT.

- You used the VISION BOX to get your prospect to spell out exactly what he or she wanted, creating a box of deliverables as opposed to trying to develop a proposal based on a more abstract vision. To accomplish this, you stayed low on the ladder of abstraction to get your prospect to describe in concrete terms what he or she would like to see happen.

- You gave the prospect a REPLAY of that vision, to confirm that you understood what he or she wanted, implying that you were the best person to deliver it.

- Instead of doing a trial close, you waved a WHITE FLAG, getting your prospect to invite you in.

- Once you got invited in, you guided your prospect through a REHEARSAL of firing your competition. You determined that your prospect had the authority and the willingness to act; and you acknowledged your prospect's decision by saying, *"So it's done."*

The Conversation

With practice, you should soon be able to recall and use the six steps of The Wedge Sales Call as easily as remembering to say please and thank you. Because The Wedge is prospect-focused and adaptable to each situation, it is an easier format to remember than a canned sales presentation. Most of the salespeople I have trained have found the conversational phrases of The Wedge Sales Call fairly easy to remember and to adjust to their own style. The phrases sound mundane but, as we have seen, each one is designed to elicit a powerful psychological response on the part of your prospect. The Wedge is as powerful as it is disarming. Let's go over the phrases for the six steps one more time:

> PICTURE PERFECT: *"I'm curious. When you receive* [a specific service] *so that you don't have to worry about* [a specific pain], *are you comfortable with that process?"*
>
> TAKE AWAY: *"Well, perhaps it's not that important because* [insert a reason].*"*
>
> VISION BOX: *"In regard to* [area of concern], *what would you like to see happen?"*

REPLAY: *"Here's what I'm hearing you say you want.* [Repeat what the prospect said.] *Have I got that right?"*

WHITE FLAG: *"So, what would you like me to do?"*

REHEARSAL: *"That's the easy part. May we talk about the hard part? . . . How will you tell your other rep that it's over? . . .*

    "Are you comfortable with everything? So it's done. Great. I'll get to work."

If you're like me and don't have a photographic memory, let me suggest a couple of practical exercises that have helped other salespeople become comfortable more quickly using The Wedge. First, beginning tomorrow, take a little time in the morning to handwrite a Wedge script including a PICTURE PERFECT question. This exercise will help you memorize the key conversational segues, as well as anticipate the things that your prospects will typically say. Second, find someone you can role-play with. Practice The Wedge Sales Call a few hours a week for the next two months. Do these two things, and you should be well on your way to using The Wedge with ease and confidence.

In Part III, I tell the story of how The Wedge was developed. We take a look at what The Wedge has done for the companies and individual sales professionals who have been using it. After that, two special chapters—one for prospects and one for current providers—look at The Wedge through the eyes of the other two parties in the selling situation. Finally, we put everything together in a brief review of strategy and tactics.

PART

III

CHANGING THE
WAY SELLING
IS DONE

CHAPTER

7

Individual Success

The extent to which The Wedge has already made a difference in the lives of so many sales professionals has been extremely gratifying. I have seen people use The Wedge to make the transition from working long hours and earning less to working smarter and earning more, giving themselves more time to be with their families, and the means to get more from their lives.

People often ask me how and when The Wedge was developed. Actually, it was crystallized out of the thousands of hours I spent asking salespeople questions about how they do what they do. The insights on which The Wedge is based did not just come out of the blue. They came from the questions I kept putting to salespeople over and over. I believe this is a major reason for the success of The Wedge. It is more than a model. It is a proven system wrought from actual sales experience. It arose from and reflects the best practices of successful producers, as well as the everyday language used by salespeople in their conversations with prospects.

Although The Wedge is an effective selling strategy across industries and professions, it was first developed from the experiences of commercial property and casualty insurance agents.

How The Wedge Was Developed

Those of you who sell insurance know how challenging it can be. And if you think selling insurance is tough, try being a buyer. To most buyers, everything looks alike. There's a lack of differentiation in buyers' minds from agency to agency, company to company, and policy to policy. Insurance to them is pretty much just insurance. It's all basically the same.

So this is one of the two big problems that agents confront. The other problem is that, most of the time, someone else already has the prospect's account. In particular, commercial property casualty insurance is a tough business. The typical agent in commercial lines enjoys a client retention rate of well over 90 percent.

When I started formulating the Wedge process in the early 1990s, I had a portfolio of insurance clients. I would talk to agent after agent and hear the same story. They called on a prospect. They had a good rapport. They listened carefully to their prospect. They put together a great proposal at a great price. They brought it back to the prospect. Everything looked good. Then, a few days later, they learned they had not gotten the business. You know what happened, of course. They got rolled by the current agent. For commercial insurance agents and for most other people in sales, the current agent, I came to recognize, was the single biggest obstacle to winning new business. This was the seed (the critical role of the current provider) that later germinated into The Wedge (the tactical process for taking out the provider, and for taking out your competitors if you are vying for an open account).

One of the questions I had been trying to answer was how to get your prospects to see what they are not getting without saying anything bad about your competition. Traditional selling, and all of the sales books I had read, did not address this dilemma with any specific solution. It was one of those sales barriers that traditional selling works around or deals with only conceptually, leaving it to the salesperson to figure out how to break through the barrier on a case-by-case basis.

With access to so many insurance agents, I worked with them to look more deeply into the words they were using in their sales calls, and the selling techniques they were employing. A typical conversation I had with an agent went something like this:

> *R.S.:* "Why do you believe you're going to win this account?"
>
> *Agent:* "Well, we're better."
>
> *R.S.:* "How are you better?"
>
> *Agent:* "We have better service."
>
> *R.S.:* "How is your service better? Everybody says that."
>
> *Agent:* "We're more responsive."
>
> *R.S.:* "Okay, that's good. Now let me ask you this: How are you going to get your prospects to see that you are more responsive, and that your competitors are not as responsive, *without your saying anything bad about them?*"

Gradually, through trial and error, based on agent selling experiences in the field, we came up with the sequence we call PICTURE PERFECT. An example would be:

"I'm curious, when your agent comes out to see you six months before renewal, and he does a midterm review to

identify and control losses and reduce costs, and to make sure your claims reserves aren't set too high, are you comfortable with that process?"

In its construction, the question appeared to break through this major sales barrier. It brought up the competition, and it brought up a pain the prospect had because of a lack of service. At the same time, by assuming that the proactive services were already being provided, the salesperson was not attacking the competition. Plus, by suggesting that these services should be done routinely, the salesperson was able to communicate "I do this kind of service" without sounding like a traditional salesperson.

The more we tested PICTURE PERFECT in the field, the more it worked. It was helping agents advance to the stage of getting their prospects to think about how they were being underserved. The next step was to create a clear, specific tactical process that would enable agents to lead their prospects into firing their current agents or ruling out other contenders in order to hire them—not just another selling concept, but a step-by-step process that agents could quickly learn and use.

We had three objectives. First, we wanted to identify the best techniques to use that would take the least amount of time. Prospects are busy people. For that matter, so are salespeople. Second, we wanted to strengthen and refine each tactical step just as we had done in perfecting the PICTURE PERFECT question. Third, we wanted to keep trying our approaches in the field, so we could gain proof that we had identified something new, beyond traditional selling, that worked better than traditional selling.

As we met these objectives, the remaining five steps of The Wedge Sales Call were developed and perfected. This is a key strength of The Wedge. It is a tactical road map that fits any sales situation where, in order for you to win, someone has to lose. Because the process is codified, it can be practiced like a golf swing. Salespeople can be trained in it, and if they can master it, they can become champions at it.

Working Smarter

It is human nature, and the desire of every salesperson I know, to want to earn more money with fewer hours of labor. It is not a matter of sloth or greed. It is a matter of efficiency. We want to get the job done and help others, and then we want to have the time to enjoy the fruits of our labors.

When I say The Wedge enables you to work smarter, I am not trying to woo you into using it with a promise of "get rich quick." There are realistic, practical reasons that The Wedge will enable you to work smarter.

Bigger, Better Prospects

Once you have a strategy for taking out your competition, you can go after not just prospects who are actively shopping but companies you previously did not even consider prospects because they had a provider in place. In many industries, that means multiplying your potential targets tenfold, and then picking the best ones rather than what traditional selling would identify as the most available ones. There is a vast hidden market out there that The Wedge enables you to reach. In effect, you can use The Wedge to create new opportunities for yourself. It enlarges the meaning of the word *prospect*.

Focused Research

If you are a well-prepared sales professional and pride yourself on finding out about your prospects before you meet with them, the Wedge precall research strategy will save you a lot of time. You can focus your research where it counts—on identifying your strengths and your competition's weaknesses regarding proactive service. Those are the competitive advantages that you will be using to win, not your mastery of the company's annual report or its latest 10-K. Remember what we said about information versus knowledge? Everyone these days has access to billions and billions of bytes of information about the companies whose business they want. The advantage goes to those salespeople who seek out the knowledge that individuals have concerning a company's day-to-day operations and its frustrations with its current service. The account goes to those salespeople who use that knowledge intelligently by converting it into powerful differentiation.

A Shortened Selling Cycle

The conversational phrases used in The Wedge Sales Call were crafted to say much more in far less time. They help you deal with the reality that your prospect is busy and that you want to use your own time wisely as well. The best Wedge practitioners in the right situations have taken prospects from rapport to rehearsal in less than an hour. Now *that* is shortening the selling cycle! The Wedge is not inconsistent with relationship selling. It simply reduces the courtship to a fraction of the time that it otherwise would take for you to bond with your prospect and win the business.

Making Winning More Predictable

Above all, The Wedge will help you make winning more predictable. What exactly does that mean? It means you can boost your closing ratio. Would you rather make 10 sales calls or five sales calls in order to win three accounts? Would you rather keep trying different sales call strategies until something clicks, or master a process that has been proven to get results time after time?

These are some of the things that enable you to work smarter using The Wedge; and once you start working smarter, you can begin earning more.

Earning More

I have not read a book on selling that did not attempt to motivate its readers with the lure of earning more. Let me say this about The Wedge. The Wedge in and of itself will not increase your earnings. You are the one who has to do that. Your effort will make the difference, and only you can put forth that effort—not me, and not this book.

However, I can tell you this: If you learn The Wedge, if you practice it and put it to work for yourself, the probability that you will earn significantly more is extremely high. To date, I have not met any competent salesperson who has used The Wedge correctly and has not achieved good results. And many have achieved great results.

I often suggest to the salespeople I coach that there are five areas where they can most productively spend their time using the Wedge approach to increase their earnings.

The Five Money-Making Activities of Salespeople

1. *Overserving the top 20 percent of your accounts, using a written service time line.*

   Once again, we find Pareto's law at work. In many businesses, 20 percent of the customers tend to generate 80 percent of the revenue. If your income depends on retaining a portfolio of clients, keeping your biggest clients pain-free is one of the surest ways not to jeopardize the higher net income that The Wedge has made it possible for you to earn.

2. *Leveraging the top 20 percent of your accounts for personal introductions to your other top prospects.*

   Your client base is a major asset at your disposal to leverage for additional business. Too many sales-people see their accounts as merely a source of current revenue, not as an asset to use for additional income. For every personal relationship you have with a client, that client has personal relationships with people who can become your prospects.

3. *Spending time on precall strategy to ensure the most effective use of your competitive advantage.*

Sales calls are trips to the plate, not batting practice. They count, and they are costly when unsuccessful. The more time you spend drilling down, finding the specific things you do better, and putting them into concrete chunks that your prospects can visualize, the better your chances of winning each deal.

4. *Going out on sales calls and, of course, winning.*

While it would not be smart to play the numbers game and conclude that the time you spend in front of prospects correlates directly with the amount of new business you win, it is useful to make sure you keep your pipeline full. A good test is to ask yourself: Is what I am currently doing related directly to either winning a specific new account or keeping or growing one of my big clients? If the answer is no, take an honest look at how you are spending your time.

5. *Cross-selling and rounding out your accounts to increase your revenue per client.*

Your client base is not only a source for introductions to prospects. It is an asset that you can cultivate and grow. Like the other four moneymaking activities, cross-selling your current clients contributes directly to increasing your income.

Ideally, a salesperson would spent about 80 percent of his or her working time on these five activities. What we have found in our interviews with salespeople is that many

144

of them spend only about 20 percent of their time on the five moneymaking activities.

If you are willing to make a concerted effort to prioritize your time as indicated, and if you are also willing to learn and practice The Wedge, you should be able to make a whole lot more money than you may have previously thought was a realistic goal for yourself. Using The Wedge, ordinary people have been achieving extraordinary results.

CHAPTER 8

The Wedge Sales Culture

Earlier we looked at how selling is not a solo sport but a contact sport. In the real world, you are out there competing against other people and, even when there is no current provider, you are usually competing against others who want to win the same accounts you do.

Selling, within your own company, is best executed as a team sport—where everyone on your sales force works together to make sure that each individual has the benefit of the varied strengths and knowledge of his or her colleagues and, in turn, that your team gets the best out of each individual.

The creation of The Wedge and the difference it was making in the lives of individual salespeople led my associates and me to wonder if this strategy could be integrated into the corporate culture of a company. What if a business could create and sustain a selling system based on The Wedge that would enable it to continue to drive growth with everyone on board?

For several years after refining the Wedge process, we would go out into the field and conduct a two-day training event with a client, showing its salespeople how to use The Wedge. Six months later, we would call back to see how things were going with the client.

"Three of our people really liked it, and are doing great," the client would say.

"And what about your other 15 reps?" we would ask.

"Well, change is hard," the client would reply.

Along the way, we had developed two other programs. One of them, Red Hot Introductions, was a process for getting your best clients to introduce you to your top prospects. The other was the CRISP sales meeting format I mentioned earlier in Chapter 2, a way of making your sales meetings a catalyst for driving growth. Up to this point, however, we had never really had a business owner ready to take the full plunge—to take all of the tools we had developed and put them together in a company-wide program.

So we kept taking our clients' money, hoping things would get better. And one day they did.

Launching The Wedge Sales Culture

The late Douglas B. Owen was a senior vice president with Summit Global Partners, a Dallas-based corporation that today is one of the 25 largest insurance brokerage, risk management, and benefits consulting firms in the country. One day, Doug came out to see me at our offices outside Dallas. He had a goal of creating a common sales culture for Summit Global and its then 15 locations. It was the first time I had had the right kind of conversation with someone who wanted to expand his or her horizons and use the Wedge strategy to develop a complete selling system for a business. For the next six hours, the two of us put the Wedge tools and programs into one consolidated format. We mapped it out, talked through it, desktopped it, put together a plan, and then edited the plan. By the time we finished, Doug had a proposal for his CEO that he believed in as much as I did. He sold it, and Summit Global contracted with us.

For the first time, we got the chance to work with an entire organization, going beyond merely doing sales training. We started with Summit Global's executives, getting a vision of where they wanted to take the company and the growth they wanted to achieve. We knew that if we could not get the top people focused, the program wouldn't be driven. Next, we trained the sales managers on how to run sales meetings in a way that would truly drive growth as an integral part of the corporate culture of the company. We then worked with the salespeople, training them in using their competitive advantage, Summit Global's proactive services, to create differentiation and win accounts away from competitors. We showed them how to use The Wedge Sales Call to win more new business faster. We trained them in Red Hot Introductions, showing them how to get their top clients to introduce them to their most desirable prospects. Finally, we followed up with a course for the customer service people to get them on the same page with everyone else.

Twelve months later, Doug was writing a memo to his CEO, summarizing the results. He noted that a year before he had contracted with The Wedge Group expecting a 10:1 return on investment (ROI). Instead, he noted, the ROI was 20:1. In one year, Summit Global had gone from annual sales of around $50 million to a new high of $97 million. The same group of people that was there when we started had been able to nearly double its sales in 12 months.

Until I saw Doug's memo, I did not realize how well Summit Global had been doing. I made a commitment the day I saw his memo that this is the way we would always do it, and we would call it The Wedge Sales Culture.

The other early adopter we worked with in implementing The Wedge Sales Culture was Higginbotham & Associates, an insurance brokerage headquartered in Fort Worth, Texas. Rusty Reid, the president and CEO of Higginbotham, had been with us as a flagship client. We had a good relationship. Rusty was a believer in The Wedge, as well as an enthusiastic, top-notch executive. Over a seven-year period, Higginbotham grew its sales from around $40 million to more than $270 million. It became one of the nation's 100 largest insurance brokerages, and in 2002 was named Commercial Insurance Agency of the Year by the National Underwriter Company.

One of the most powerful things about the Higginbotham story is that the company has one of the highest hit ratios for new salespeople in the industry. The producers who come aboard at Higginbotham thrive on The Wedge Sales Culture that is already in place when they arrive. It shortens their learning curve, and gets them up to speed much faster. Out of 23 new salespeople added to the Higginbotham staff in the most recent five years, 22 have stuck it out and are successful, reaching or exceeding their sales goals.

The success of Higginbotham and Summit Global confirmed for us that The Wedge is more than a selling strategy for individual salespeople. It is the basis for a sales culture that a company can create and sustain in order to drive growth—a selling system that can be replicated for

151

any business whose profitable growth depends on sales and, especially, on getting its competition fired.

Creating The Wedge Sales Culture for Your Company

If I were talking to your company about The Wedge Sales Culture, I might share with you a story that a management consultant I know likes to tell. It's about General Dwight D. Eisenhower at the time Ike took command of the Allied forces in World War II. As the story goes, Ike took a piece of string and laid it on the table. Pulling the string along the table, he pointed out how the entire string glided along, fully aligned and straight. Then he pushed the string, which curled up and went nowhere. His goal was to illustrate that an organization is successful when its people are pulling together in a common direction, not when individuals are pushing with no common vision.

At my home, we have horses. One of our largest is Commander, and one of his stable mates is Ladybug, who is smaller. If I hitched them together facing in opposite directions, Commander would have a heck of a time dragging Ladybug around. However, if I joined them as a team and pointed them in the same direction, their horsepower would increase dramatically.

It is the same way in business. If you work for a company, you know what I am talking about. It can seem at times as if you have two competing systems in place at the office pulling in different directions. On the one hand, you try to operate according to the rules of the marketplace.

These rules tell you to focus on high quality, low cost, speed, and innovation. This is the formal policy of your firm, and of many others. On the other hand, at work every day you are part of an informal culture. Unlike the business rules, the cultural rules are based on social factors, office politics, and personalities. When these two systems are out of whack, your best-laid plans go awry. If you are in a commission-driven environment, the results can be downright paralyzing at times. When everyone is not pulling in the same direction, human foibles will come to the surface in the form of personality clashes, turf battles, backstabbing, and lack of confidence in management. These soft factors soon show up in your hard numbers such as turnover, profitability, and revenue. The point is that there are many things not directly considered to be sales-related that nevertheless can have a major impact on sales.

When people come together as an organization, they need a common vision that unites them in the pursuit of common goals. Each of them needs to feel as if he or she is a stakeholder in the outcome of the group's performance. Without this unity, communications are ambiguous, misunderstandings arise, performance suffers, and sales falter.

The purpose of The Wedge Sales Culture is to create and sustain alignment around a common vision, and to put in place a selling system based on The Wedge that will outlive employees who come and go. More than that, The Wedge Sales Culture is designed to put a business on track for turbocharged growth by incorporating the strategy and tactics of The Wedge into everything it does. In short, it is a way of doing business that your company can use to make winning more predictable by getting your competition fired.

Aligning the Four Groups of a Company

If your company is like most, you have four major categories of personnel: (1) executives, (2) middle management including sales management, (3) sales producers, and (4) customer support staff. The first step in creating The Wedge Sales Culture is to get these four groups into alignment.

Notre Dame football fans are familiar with the legendary Four Horsemen who led them to the national championship in 1925. Harry Stuhldreher, the quarterback, was the *executive* on the field, a self-assured leader who inspired his fellow players. Left halfback Jim Crowley was a super middle *manager*, running cleverly with the ball when Stuhldreher handed it off to him. Right halfback Don Miller was a star *producer*, a major breakaway threat when he got an opportunity. The fullback, Elmer Laden, was a terrific *support* player who also shined on defense with timely interceptions and in handling punting chores when needed.

On their own, they were unlikely heroes. None of them weighed more than 162 pounds, and none of them stood more than six feet tall. Yet, when they worked together, they became what some sports fans consider one of the greatest backfields in college football history.

When your players are aligned, your company can do extraordinary things as well. Your executives can inspire and lead the way; your managers can make sure that productivity is kept at a consistently high level; your producers can thrive and bring in new business; and your customer service people can make sure your clients are kept happy and opportunities are not missed.

The Wedge Sales Culture is a game plan for achieving this result—and it begins with giving everyone involved a reason to care, an incentive to change.

The Five-Step Change Formula

Change in an organization begins with *vision*. It involves taking action to become something in the future that you are not today. Next, you need a *strategy* to achieve your vision, a plan for reaching the goals you set. Third, you need to convert that strategy into *routines and habits* that people perform daily. After that, you need to reinforce success by *celebrating* and rewarding accomplishment. Finally, you need to maintain a *cultural network*, a shared pool of knowledge, belief, and behavior that current employees can pass along to new employees. A company that achieves all five steps—vision, strategy, routines and habits, celebrating, and cultural network—will have put a sales culture in place that is far more likely to last.

When I am talking to executives and managers about The Wedge Sales Culture, I often use the example of a person on a diet to explain the challenge. If this does not apply to you, then you have my congratulations and my envy. Most of us, however, do need to think about calories. Suppose, then, that you have decided to lose 20 pounds.

That is your vision. It is how you see yourself in the future. You see you, 20 pounds lighter. To achieve your vision, you need a strategy. So you decide to eat better, cutting back on the wrong kinds of carbohydrates. You also decide to exercise. Without time to commit to a gym, you buy a treadmill and put it in your bedroom at home.

For eight weeks, everything is going great. You wake up in the morning, and jog on your treadmill while watching the news on CNN. You cut back on your carbs, and you start to see the pounds come off. Then, however, you go on a vacation that you and your spouse have been planning. You sit on the beach, but you still manage to watch what you eat and to run beside the surf now and then. When you get back to the office, you have a "to do" list waiting for you. While you catch up, you start to save a little time by skipping the treadmill every now and then. You get busier at the office and one day you grab a fast-food lunch, telling yourself that you will not make a habit of it. Before long, however, the treadmill sits on your floor unused, your eating choices regress, and you step on the scale one morning and find that you have gained back most of those lost pounds. What happened? Your routine died. That killed your strategy. And that, in turn, killed your vision.

That is how most traditional sales training works. It is why I tell my clients that most sales training is a waste of money. It is akin to taking an obese person who works at an ice cream parlor, sending that person to Jenny Craig, and then putting the person right back at the ice cream parlor again. If the environment has not changed, the people in the environment are not likely to change, either. What is the solution? It is to change the environment, to create a sales culture.

Vision

If I were speaking to your company, I would first ask you to imagine where you want to be in three years. It has surprised me to learn how many businesses do not set specific growth goals beyond the current year, if at all. What that often means is that their profitable growth, if any, will be incremental.

Having specific goals expressed in dollar terms and extending out at least three years is important for two reasons. First, a three-year vision will be a benchmark against which your company can measure its performance month to month and quarter to quarter. Second, it will be a unifying symbol that will focus everyone in your organization on your common objective—a key step in maintaining alignment among executives, managers, producers, and support staff.

Why is buy-in by all four groups so important? There is not a single individual employed by your company, full-time or part-time, who does not have some measurable impact on your success. Therefore, your people will feel ownership in your success to the degree their jobs are defined as contributing to that success. Their buy-in will help focus them on the aspects of their jobs that most directly affect sales and growth, making them more sales-conscious in the way they perform their duties.

All of this may seem elementary to you but, as mentioned, you might be surprised to find out how many businesses have no formal, announced growth goals as their vision. Without such a vision your company may not perish, but neither will it likely become a high-growth enterprise.

Strategy

Once your company has embraced a three-year vision, I would tell you that The Wedge Sales Culture demands a strategy that is different from that used by your competitors, who probably rely on traditional selling. In fact, I would tell you that your competitors are going to become a more central focus of your strategy than ever before. In most markets today, especially in competitive services markets, rapid growth requires taking accounts away from those who currently have them as well as from competitors aggressively seeking them. The strategy of The Wedge Sales Culture is aimed at achieving two objectives: (1) creating more opportunities for your salespeople to use The Wedge to win those accounts and (2) involving everyone in your organization in the pursuit and retention of new business.

When your company and its salespeople decide to go about the pursuit of new business more aggressively, your foremost problem is time. There are just so many hours in a day to get things done. This creates several challenges. How can you make the most of your limited time to win new accounts? What strategy can you put in place to maximize and use your competitive advantage to achieve rapid growth? Moreover, how many accounts of what size should you be handling to increase your profit? Which accounts should you overserve, leave to your customer service center to handle, or consider discarding?

Our strategy to meet these challenges, incorporating The Wedge, is called Million Dollar Producer. By now, your business has decided how much growth it wants to achieve in how many years. Growth goals, of course, vary widely by industry. For example, for our property casualty insurance agency clients, we looked at how they operate and developed with many of them a goal of doubling their book of business in three years with half as many accounts. For another type of business, your three-year goal might be to achieve a 30 percent gain in revenue ($30 million added to $100 million) while increasing your number of accounts by no more than 10 percent (5 accounts added to 50 accounts).

The Million Dollar Producer strategy requires your company to do four things to accelerate your profitable sales growth: (1) *position* your business for profitability and growth, (2) *leverage* your clients for introductions to prospects, (3) *grow* your client base using The Wedge, and (4) track results on a *scoreboard* so you can analyze those results and reinforce and reward achievement.

Position

As we noted before, a fairly reliable rule of thumb for many companies is that about 20 percent of your clients account for 80 percent of your revenue. These are the 20 percent that you should be overserving. Every one of your top clients should be on a written proactive services time line. What about the 80 percent of your clients who produce 20 percent of your revenue? The top half of these can probably be handled by your customer service staff or outsourced to a customer service center. As for the bottom 40 percent of your clientele, your company needs to ask itself if serving them is a business in which you want to remain. There may be valid reasons for carrying them (obviously, for example, this principle of discarding your smallest accounts would not apply to retail businesses that sell on volume), but as a general rule it puts a drag on your performance—unless you are exceptional enough that you handle every account profitably.

Leverage

By overserving the top 20 percent of your clients, you in effect will earn the right to ask them to introduce you to top prospects whom they know personally. The clients they can introduce you to are probably very desirable. Birds of a feather flock together.

Your client base, especially the top 20 percent, is an asset that too many salespeople never leverage. When I am talking to groups of salespeople, I often ask them how many times in the past 90 days they have asked one of their best clients for an introduction to one of their best prospects. Typically, in groups of 20 to 40 people, 3 of every 20 will say that they have, and 17 will say that they have not. It could be that the reluctant 17 are not overserving their clients with a written proactive services time line and, therefore, do not believe that they have earned the right to ask. Whatever the reason, they are overlooking a major opportunity staring them in the face. There is no way into a sales call more powerful than a personal introduction. I am certain that you already know this. I make the point here because, in talking to salespeople around the country, I find that this is still not being done routinely; so let me digress briefly and talk about the program I mentioned earlier, Red Hot Introductions.

Part of the pain of being a salesperson is that, as mentioned before, you have just so much time. You would like to use that time to make more money. It takes time to identify and then get in to see the people you need to talk to. In many cases, they do not want to see you. So the first question is: How do you get to the person you need to see? Basically, there are three ways to get in to see a prospect: (1) cold calls, (2) referrals, and (3) personal introductions.

The second question is: What is the best way in? Each of the three methods has its place and its success stories, but there are differences in the time it takes for each method to yield a qualified lead that you can go in and close. Would you rather win a new account by making 100 cold calls, by getting 10 referrals, or by having someone you know introduce you personally to a major prospect that he or she knows?

When you make a cold call, you are starting from scratch with your prospect. When you are referred to a prospect by someone who knows both of you, you have gained an audience, but for all you know your prospect is simply doing the referrer a favor by seeing you. Imagine, instead, that your prospect gets a phone call from a good friend of his who says something like this:

"Hi, Dirk. This is Wayne. I just wanted to share a story with you. Two years ago, I met this guy, Henry O'Toole. I was looking for a good financial adviser, and he and I

161

seemed to click. Since then, he has been outstanding. With the market tanking, he grew my portfolio 25 percent. He consistently sends me helpful tips and suggestions. Every quarter he stops by personally and we go over strategy. Anyway, Dirk, I started thinking . . . if Henry can do all this for me, then why couldn't he do the same thing for a few of my closest friends? So that's why I called. If you visit with this guy, I'm telling you that you won't regret it."

Why do more salespeople not ask their clients and others for personal introductions to prospects? In his popular book *Games People Play*, psychiatrist Eric Berne describes what he calls the "Yes But" game. Many people who know that something is the best thing to do, Dr. Berne explains, will come up with an excuse not to do it, and that excuse usually is rooted in some unfounded fear.

In my firm's own research on selling habits, we have found the same thing. Many of the salespeople we interview are playing the same kinds of head games. Do any of these characters sound like you or like someone with whom you work?

> *Mr. Professional:* "I'd ask Jim to get me in to see the guy, but I don't want to look like I can't do it myself."
>
> *Ms. Contented:* "I'm already making enough. Why push it?"
>
> *Mr. Undeserving:* "I've done my job for Linda, but what's so outstanding about my work that gives me the right to ask her?"

Ms. Delay: "I don't know the right time to ask. How do I know when to bring it up? How long should I have worked for a client before asking?"

Mr. Pessimist: "I've tried doing that before, but it doesn't work."

Ms. Quid Pro Quo: "I could ask Lennie, but what's in it for him?"

Mr. Status Quo: "I know Carl would help, but I don't want to jeopardize a good relationship."

Ms. Proud: "Yes, I can call Edgar, but I don't want him to think I need a handout to make enough."

Mr. Humble: "Jack knows how well I'm doing. I'd ask him, but I don't want to look greedy."

Ms. Inexperienced: "I've never done it before. How would I?"

We also have found in our research that clients have their own hang-ups about making personal introductions. First, although their salesperson has solved a unique problem for them, they cannot readily think of someone they know who might need the same thing. Second, some clients feel that their salesperson is a nice individual and has done a good job, but not a truly exceptional job. They do not want their friends to think they have introduced them to someone who is run-of-the-mill. Third, while the salesperson is considered trustworthy, he or she has not gained the total trust and confidence of the client. The client is not sure what the salesperson would do in a different situation.

With mental blocks on both sides of the table, you obviously need something to jump-start the process. When you work for clients, what do they most favorably remember about your service? What stands out in their minds? What really triggers the pleasure centers of their brains and gets their endorphins flowing? What excites them about your work? Remember, getting the job done is not exceptional. Neither is responding to client problems. Nor is doing what your client asked you to do. What is it, then, that turns your satisfied client into a passionate partisan? As I discussed earlier, it is your proactive, extraordinary service that makes the difference—the things you do without being asked, anticipating your client's future needs and preventing problems before they arise.

The question then becomes: How do you get your clients to agree to make Red Hot Introductions? Equally important, how do get them to do it in a way that presents you to prospects in the best light? We have a process that we call The Six Steps to a Red Hot Introduction:

Let us say that you have decided to ask Paul, your client of three years, to introduce you to prospects he knows. You want to make sure that Paul calls them, and that he introduces you to each of them in a way that will make them *want* to see you. You have a meeting scheduled with Paul tomorrow on another matter, so you decide to do it then. Now it is time to go over the conversation you will have with Paul tomorrow, the six steps.

Step 1 will be to bring up the topic with Paul. During a lull in your conversation, or as you have finished talking about the other business at hand, you will have your chance to change the subject. A story is a natural way to create this transition. You can use a story to give Paul a valid reason why you are asking for his help. Any one of three kinds of stories will fit your purpose: (1) a personal story about yourself, (2) a business story about yourself, or (3) a story about the prospects you want.

A Personal Story.   One valid reason for asking Paul for help is money. Of course, some salespeople are uncomfortable with this. As we discussed, you may have a concern about appearing to be needy or greedy. In this case, you can link the need for income to someone else. For example:

> *"You know, Paul, my wife and I have three kids. We were talking the other day about how we're going to put them through college. So I decided it's time to step up the pace. The kind of clients I'm looking for are . . ."*

A Business Story.   If you are uneasy talking about your personal life, you can use a business story:

> *"Things in business have really changed, haven't they, Paul? Everybody's trying to be more productive with fewer people. It's happened with us, too—pressure from the top for each person to bring in more. So I was thinking about the types of clients who make the most sense. For example . . ."*

A Third-Party Story.   If you are not comfortable talking about why *you* need the introduction, you can talk about the prospects whom you would like to help in the same way that you helped Paul:

> *"It's interesting, Paul, the more I'm in this business the more I run into people who are in the same situation you were in three years ago when we first talked. Not your competitors, but other kinds of companies such as [A] and [B]. I guess the firms we can most help would be . . ."*

By using a story, you will give yourself the segue you need. Then you can smoothly continue the conversation. Paul will understand where you are coming from. Like most people, he has a natural instinct to be helpful for the right reason.

Step 2 will be to get Paul focused on the kinds of prospects you most want. You know that he has contacts with a lot of businesses, but you cannot expect him to do your work for you by analyzing them and deciding which ones are the best fit for you. Nor do you want to settle for whatever companies are on the top of Paul's mind—misfits included. So you will help Paul by giving him your ideal prospect profile:

> *"The companies I'm talking about would have annual sales of, say, $50 million or higher. Their industry niche would be [A], and they'd offer services like [B] and [C]."*

At this point, Paul may tilt his head up and put his hand on his chin, trying to come up with a few names. So you will help him identify the companies.

Step 3, therefore, will be to describe your best-case

scenario to Paul—the type of business, its size or income, its needs that you can meet, and any other factors that make it an ideal match for you and what you offer. You can use this profile to jog Paul's memory, and get him thinking about the people he knows whose businesses fit your description.

As Paul flips through his mental Rolodex, you can start throwing out some names to be helpful:

> *"I was thinking, for example, Southeast Distributors and Karamazov Brothers Wholesale. Do you know any folks at either of these companies?"*

Prior to seeing Paul, you already will have used your ideal prospect profile to create your own Top 20 prospects list. If you are going to leverage your relationship with Paul, it only makes sense to start with the most desirable potential clients. If you have memorized your Top 20 list, you can keep throwing out examples until some of them hit. When they do, you will be ready to pop the question to Paul.

Step 4 will be to ask for the call. And how did you get in a position to ask Paul to pick up the phone and make the call? You earned the right to ask, you motivated Paul to be helpful, by giving him proactive, extraordinary service. This laid the groundwork for your being able to leverage your relationship with Paul. It will give him more confidence that the prospects he calls will end up regarding his call as a favor he did for them rather than as a favor they did for him. So you will say to Paul:

> *"Paul, would you be willing to call Southeast? You know, tell them what we've done for you, and see if they'd like to talk?"*

167

If the prospect is local, you can ask Paul to suggest that you and the prospect meet for lunch. If the prospect is out of town, Paul can pave the way for a phone call from you. So you anticipate that Paul will be willing to make the call. Done deal? Not yet.

Step 5 will be to coach Paul on what to say. You will ask:

"I'm just curious, Paul. What do you think is the best thing to tell Southeast?"

Paul likely will reply that he intends to tell Southeast what a great job you have done. After all, the CEO at Southeast knows him, he will explain. But will this make the CEO eager to see you? Likely not. So you will help Paul help you, by tactfully prepping him on what to say—a message that will differentiate you with specific, concrete words that will fire up the CEO when Paul calls him. Remember the ladder of abstraction we discussed earlier? Here is one more instance where it increases your power of persuasion. The more that you can help your clients visualize the concrete details of your proactive service, the easier it will be for them to communicate your strengths to others.

SODAR is an acronym for a five-step process that you can use to jog Paul's memory about what a great job you have done, rehearse him to introduce you in the best possible way, and make sure he calls and reports back to you on the results. Here are the five steps of SODAR:

1. *Situation.*
    "Remember your situation when we met, Paul? The issues that made you consider working with us?"

2. *Opportunity.*

"How did you see us as an opportunity? I mean, how did you think we could help you? Was it the problem you had, and how we approached solving it?"

3. *Decision.*

"And when you made the decision to hire us, how did you assess us? Is there one thing that really stands out in your mind?"

4. *Action.*

"How has it gone since then? Did we take the right action? Do you remember the specific steps we took to improve things?"

5. *Results.*

"And what were the results? Did they affect the bottom line? Productivity? Sales? Efficiency? Can you quantify the difference it made, guesstimate a number?"

Once you take Paul through SODAR, he can effectively recommend you rather than merely refer you. He can tell the CEO at Southeast a real story, not merely generalize to him that you are a sharp person and maybe you can do him some good.

Step 6 will be to make sure that Paul follows through. While you want Paul to make the call sooner rather than later, it might be counterproductive to push him. So you give him the courtesy of choosing the time. You ask:

"When would be a good time to call you back, Paul, to hear how it went?"

When Paul suggests that you call him next Tuesday, you will have accomplished two things: (1) Paul will have agreed to call before a specific deadline; and (2) he will have given you the opportunity to follow up, to make sure he made the call, and to hear the results. Before Paul makes the call, you can send him a brief e-mail, expressing your appreciation and reviewing the key points that you brought out with SODAR. When you call Paul back on Tuesday, he can fill you in on the call and pass along any timely information he learned when he talked to your prospect.

To this point, we have talked about how to position your business for profitability and growth, and how to leverage your clients for introductions to prospects. The next part of the Million Dollar Producer strategy is to grow your client base more rapidly using The Wedge.

Growth

As discussed in Chapter 2, there are three basic dimensions of competition: price, product, and service. Most companies do not have a strong competitive advantage when it comes to price, product, and reactive service. These days it is your company's proactive service that can make all the difference in winning new accounts. Your proactive services platform gives you a strong story to tell about your business; and it gives you the concrete, visual examples you need to use The Wedge to get your competition fired. In a very real sense, your proactive services platform can drive your company's growth. The question is: Does your company have a strategy to ensure that you are using this competitive advantage to drive growth? Do you have a system in place to make sure that every sales call is as potent as it can be?

On hundreds of occasions in my career I have been the outside party attending a company's sales meeting. It has always struck me how much time salespeople spend in these rituals for little or no gain. You know what I am talking about. I am sure you have sat impatiently through one of these sessions as prospect lists are rehashed, personal stories are told, unfocused opinions are muttered, and the person presiding gives lip service at the close of the meeting to everyone's general resolve to get out there and win more business.

It remains my view that the sales meeting is one of the most underutilized resources for growth that a company has. Yet, if done the right way, your sales meeting can be a powerful catalyst for driving sales. I spoke earlier about the CRISP (continuous and rapid improvement sales process) sales meeting. As part of The Wedge Sales Culture, the very purpose of the CRISP sales meeting is to drive growth. For that reason, its agenda is strictly limited to four topics: (1) how to get introductions to specific prospects; (2) what specific new business appointments have been set; (3) what specific proposals have been submitted and are pending; and (4) what specific deals have been closed and, therefore, are cause to celebrate.

The CRISP sales meeting format requires that everyone attending stay focused on new business, and new business only. Instead of being passive listeners, your producers and others attending can help each other strategize how to use The Wedge for each new business

171

interview—developing specific Wedges to use, sharing any intelligence they have on each specific prospect and its decision makers, and otherwise contributing directly to moving each deal forward in the selling process. This is how your sales team and company can use sales meetings to enhance your ability to break prospects' relationships with your competitors and grow faster.

Now that we have talked about positioning your business for growth, leveraging your clients for introductions, and growing your client base using The Wedge, let me go over the fourth part of the Million Dollar Producer strategy: keeping score.

Scoreboard

Jack Welch was a remarkable leader during his days at General Electric in creating a high-growth, high-profit culture. One of the things he believed intensely was that if you cannot measure it, you cannot control it. When you track your company's growth, there will be certain numbers within your overall growth that it makes strategic sense for you to keep an eye on. You know the types of numbers I am talking about—the closing ratio for your sales force and for each of your salespeople; your average revenue per relationship; how many accounts you are winning; what portion of your new business is "new" new as opposed to cross-sold; and any other numbers that bear on whether your growth is profitable, marginal, or merely a wash in terms of your overall net income. The point is that the more you know, the more you can measure; the more you can measure, the more you can control; and the more you can control, the more predictable you can make winning.

Let us assume that your company now has a vision, as well as a strategy to achieve that vision. The third part of the five-step change formula, routines and habits, is where the rubber meets the road. Only by converting your strategy into routines and habits that people perform daily can you make things happen.

Routines and Habits

My four young daughters did not always regularly brush their teeth without prompting from my wife and me. It took repetition plus a little friendly encouragement before they started doing it automatically. Most of us are open to learning new things, but it takes even more motivation and persistence to keep doing those things consistently until they become habits and routines.

When your company has a vision of where it wants to go and a strategy to get it there, the question becomes: How are we going to implement this thing called The Wedge Sales Culture? How are we going to get our people to do what they need to do to make it work?

Your Sales Management Team

The structure of a typical company that we have been talking about—executives, managers, salespeople, and service staff—creates a nice organization chart. It tells you the bureaucratic pecking order. It shows you who reports to

173

whom. It describes how your e-mail and paperwork are routed and distributed. When you gaze at it, your company looks like a well-organized machine. But does this chart really show you how selling gets done? Does it show you who will drive The Wedge Sales Culture until it becomes a habit and a routine for people?

In the traditional business model, your sales managers are the linchpins. They report to your executives, and they mentor and direct your salespeople. They are the lightning rods, getting more credit when things go well and more blame when things go badly than they probably deserve. When your company implements The Wedge Sales Culture—when your executives, managers, salespeople, and support staff have embraced your vision and accepted the strategy—a different kind of sales management team will emerge.

In working with companies that choose to create The Wedge Sales Culture, I have found that four key roles are vital in implementing it and making things happen. The job titles of the people in these roles may vary, but the roles—and the personality types that go with them—are very similar from one company to the next. Seldom will any of these four roles be exclusively vested in one person. More commonly, several people will perform each role, with one of them emerging as the most frequent leader.

1. *The culture creator*. This is the person who keeps the vision alive. Often, it is the owner or chief executive, but it can be a vice president or someone else down the line. During the Apollo XIII drama, for example,

it was the flight director, Gene Krantz, and not the head of NASA, who stepped up and said, "Failure is not an option." The culture creator is the person who personifies and promotes your sales culture, communicates expectations, motivates the troops, rallies everyone to the growth goals, and leads the way.

2. *The coach/mentor.* This person is all about helping others. He or she is not into self-aggrandizement. The coach/mentor encourages, counsels, and supports. The person in this role listens carefully at the CRISP sales meeting, and then follows up to help your salespeople close the deals that were discussed. The coach/mentor is like a third base coach in baseball, telling players "You can do it!" as they head for home.

3. *The product manager.* The person in this role discovers what clients want, and responds with services and products. He or she keeps a close watch on the marketplace, what your company is offering, and how you are delivering your service. On one day, you might find the product manager working with your customer support staff to build your proactive services platform; and on another day, he or she will be shaping your offering to take advantage of buying trends and new opportunities. In many industries today, the ability to niche market has become one of the most dependable paths to growth, making this role even more important. Internally, the product manager is an integrator, getting everyone on the same page day-to-day to ensure that you are making the most of your competitive advantage.

175

4. *The administrator.* This person is a chronicler, numbers person, and analyst. He or she tracks your growth, gives progress reports, notes trends and warning signs, and offers insights based on mastery of the data. The administrator is a logical, detail-oriented person, more like Mr. Spock than Captain Kirk aboard your enterprise. He or she is the go-to person for anyone who asks, "How are we doing?" The administrator knows that you cannot chart a course without knowing where you have been, where you are, and where you are going.

This more informal sales management team, as opposed to the official sales management team on your organization chart, will be the driving force that keeps your progress on track. The people in the four roles will be major catalysts in converting your strategy into the routines and habits that make profitable growth a part of your marrow.

As mentioned earlier, The Wedge Sales Culture is about driving growth with *everyone* on board. Most companies currently have their executives and managers, and of course their producers, involved directly in sales to one degree or another. Many companies, however, make the mistake of seeing sales and service as two distinct functions. As a result, their customer support staff is not considered a part of the sales team. Worse, some service reps have an aversion to seeing themselves as salespeople at all. You know the personality type I am talking about. You stick your head in the door of your customer service center, and you ask an account executive if a client might be interested in a new service you now offer. Rather than having the answer or volunteering to call, the account exec says, "Why don't you ask them and see?"

Customer Service and Sales

Virtually all companies recognize that their salespeople are service people. What they do not always fully appreciate is that their service people are salespeople. As a result, they never fully engage their service staff in selling. Moreover, as we noted, many of their service people resist seeing themselves in a sales role.

This is all the more ironic because, as we discussed earlier, proactive customer service is your strongest competitive advantage in winning accounts away from current providers as well as in keeping your most desirable clients.

Your service staff should be emphatically welcomed aboard as part of your sales team. They should be given the training and tools they need to be able to more effectively cross-sell current clients and retain your key accounts. Our experience working with businesses has shown us that this is a very doable objective. When brought into the sales process in a way that motivates them about their role, your service people can significantly add to what your officially designated salespeople bring in. When that happens, the partition between sales and service comes down, and you truly begin driving growth with everyone on board.

When you have a vision of where you are headed, a strategy for getting there, and the routines and habits to make it feasible, you have done three of the five things you need to do to create a sales culture. The question then becomes: How do you reinforce and sustain your new way of doing business over time? Moreover, how do you ensure that your selling system is not disrupted as employees come and go? This brings us to the last two steps of the five-step change formula.

Celebrating

Imagine yourself standing on the tee box of a par three hole, playing alone on a virtually empty golf course. You hit your tee shot and it lands on the green, bounces twice, and rolls into the cup. Your first hole in one! You turn to tell somebody, and there is only silence. Nobody saw you do it. How does that feel?

Earlier in this chapter, we talked about the soft factors that can affect the hard numbers of business performance—the psychology, politics, and social dealings that come into play when you put people together in a group. My firm in 2003–2004 conducted a survey of some of our clients to study these soft factors. We selected a representative sample of 26 firms, and we asked their personnel to answer a series of questions related to how they saw their job, their employer, their colleagues, and their common mission. We then benchmarked the results against the results of top-performing companies whose personnel had taken a similar survey. Strikingly, the greatest deviation from the ideal benchmark related to how well, in the eyes of the employees we surveyed, their management was rewarding and reinforcing their productivity. It was not a matter of compensation and bonuses. As they saw it, the reinforcement that was lacking could have been simple acknowledgment for a job well done, a pat on the back more often, or some other way of celebrating success.

The result was striking for two reasons. First, celebration has been a basic instinct of people since our primitive ancestors started raising their fists in the air after hitting a wild boar with a rock from 50 feet away. Second, celebrating success is such a huge part of human culture in general. We are teeming with celebrations—the Oscars, the Emmys, sports Halls of Fame, Nobel Prizes, Pulitzer Prizes, best-dressed lists, baby's first steps, birthdays, anniversaries, and, yes, we even celebrate days of the week such as thank God it's Friday (TGIF).

It is all the more ironic, then, that so many companies do not take advantage of this morale-boosting, team-bonding activity. I know this is an obvious point, but it bears repeating as one of those easy-to-do things that a busy company can overlook to its detriment.

Even when you are celebrating the achievement of an individual, the occasion can be used to acknowledge and reinforce good performance generally. When Hank Aaron knocked his 715th home run out of the park, surpassing Babe Ruth, a supporting cast of managers, coaches, players, bat boys, and fans in the stands could each rightfully claim a share of the honor. But for the roles of these people, Aaron might have missed a homer here or there. There is an old proverb that victory has a thousand fathers and defeat is an orphan. It is a wise saying to keep in mind each time your company wins.

Your Cultural Network

Thus far, we have been talking about your business and its employees as if we were looking at a snapshot of your current personnel frozen in time. In reality, people come and go. According to the United States Bureau of Labor Statistics, the average employee now makes four to six career changes, and 12 to 15 job changes, before retiring. Moreover, the job market today puts more of a premium on flexibility, encouraging people to move around even if they are happy where they are. The final step of the five-step change formula is to put a lasting cultural network in place at your company that will be sustained as employees come aboard, go elsewhere, or switch roles within your organization.

Merriam-Webster's Collegiate Dictionary defines culture as "the integrated pattern of human knowledge, belief, and behavior that depends upon the capacity for learning and transmitting knowledge to succeeding generations." The sales process and business performance can be a little fuzzy in this regard. There are a lot of things people do intuitively that do not get written down, let alone put into a formal process. In his book, *Boyd: The Fighter Pilot Who Changed the Art of War*, author Robert Coram described the legendary exploits of the late John Boyd, an Air Force colonel who took what had been seen as the "art" of air-to-air combat and codified it into a process that other pilots could replicate and use.

That is one of the major benefits of creating a sales culture. In its distilled form, The Wedge Sales Culture consists of processes, tools, methods, and techniques that can be perpetuated and replicated. When that happens, your company's employees will find themselves sharing in a common network based on a body of "knowledge, belief, and behavior" that energizes discussions in the boardroom as well as chitchats next to the watercooler. Moreover, your company's new employees will have a network in place to tap into, shortening their learning curve as they grow into productive participants in your sales culture.

With a vision, a strategy, routines and habits, celebrations, and a cultural network in place, your company will be readier than ever to win new business like a well-run machine, adding and growing accounts as you get your competition fired.

CHAPTER

9

For Buyers Only

If you think selling is hard, try being a buyer.
                                        —Randy Schwantz

Being a buyer is one of the most difficult jobs on the planet for two obvious reasons. First, you have limited time. Second, you have limited money. Even if you had all the time in the world and an unlimited budget, it would still be a difficult job. To me, the most difficult part of being a buyer is trying to sort out the differences in products and services. Because that is so difficult, too often buyers leverage their almighty dollar to bust the chops of sellers. Why? Because the money aspect is the easiest thing to compare. Needless to say, this book has been about helping sellers do a better job of getting inside their own heads, discovering their own differences, and finding a better way to convey those differences to you, the buyer, in order to make your job easier.

Having spent many thousands of hours with sellers, I know that many of them have a very difficult time communicating their differences. Many sellers have never thought about what all those features and benefits really mean to you, the buyer. So why a chapter for you, the buyer, in a book on selling? My reason is simple. As a buyer, you have a lot to gain from helping sellers be better at communicating. Sellers have the capability to save you time, energy, and money, but I believe you have to help them use that capability.

On the Edge

I know that most sellers would be offended by my telling you this, because most of them believe they are great communicators. In many ways they are, but in some ways they aren't. So I'm going out on the edge and make a suggestion to you, the buyer, on how to get the most from the sellers calling on you.

I'm hoping that you have a whiteboard in your office. If not, then imagine that you do. I'm suggesting that, when the salesperson arrives, you conduct your part of the sales call about the same way that I conduct a sales meeting. I'm hoping that unlike most buyers, who either sit behind their power desk or politely move over to the little round table, you'll go right up to the whiteboard with a marker in your hand.

I believe that a person who runs a sales meeting should be part facilitator and part journalist. I'd encourage you to use these same skills I learned that enable me to conduct a strategy session with salespeople before they go on sales calls. So now you're up there at the whiteboard, conducting your part of a sales call with a seller who has stopped by your office.

As you know, there is an information battle going on in most seller/buyer settings. Since you as the buyer have more power, you should be more gracious in setting the tone for the meeting by reducing the information battle and talking about your own needs and wants. Too many sales calls start off with the seller's asking questions of the buyer, and with the buyer's responding in general that everything is fine except for price. I suppose that is okay,

185

but it is not much of an intellectual response from the buyer. That's why I encourage you to cut through the games, respect the time of the seller the same as your own, and immediately start the facilitation process.

I'd encourage you to move very rapidly to the whiteboard. Then, I wish you would start the interview process using your journalistic skills, and visually map out what the seller is telling you.

The buyer-seller game is interesting in that most buyers believe that the better they are at withholding information, the more power they maintain. Perhaps they do maintain power, but in the process of withholding information they lose out on effectiveness.

Let me give you an example. One of the best buyer-seller meetings I've ever had was the one I mentioned previously with Doug Owen of Summit Global Partners. Doug came to visit with me. He was a very intelligent man, very confident and willing to engage. We started the meeting with the same chitchat that most meetings start with, and then he kindly told me his objectives. He told me what he knew about his situation and what his challenges were. Unlike many buyers, he didn't pretend that things were better than they really were. He just told it like it was. He then asked my opinion about what could be done. As I began to talk, Doug moved toward the whiteboard and began mapping out my thoughts and strategies. This whole effort epitomized what I think of as collaboration, partnering, and synergy. It also helped me remain relevant to his cause.

In hindsight, I can tell you that what we did was utilize the skills from Chapter 5 on the VISION BOX. The result was a proposal that concretely matched Doug's desires, something that he could sell to his CEO with passion. The bottom line was pretty amazing. As a buyer he was very excited about what he was about to get. As a seller, I was pleased and confident in our plan of action. The results, as we noted earlier, were even more impressive, a 20:1 return on investment after he had hoped for a 10:1 return. Twelve months into the program, his expectations were more than realized.

Two Kinds of Buyers and Sellers

There is a lesson in this for all buyers and sellers. There is no doubt in my mind that there are two kinds of sellers and two kinds of buyers. There are many sellers who are BS artists. I would be on your side if you immediately threw them out of your office at the first hint or smell that they are stretching the truth and are focused purely on themselves. The other type of seller is genuine, smart, real, and interested in helping make your life better. Likewise there are buyers whose egos are so inflated that they, too, are BS artists. They withhold valuable information and play power games. I advise sellers to run from these buyers as quickly as possible. Life is too short. However, there are buyers who are very solid, genuine, forthcoming, and engaging.

I'm hoping that with the information in this book, more buyers and sellers will engage in collaborative and meaningful conversation, resulting in greater prosperity for each other, and the creation of long-term, satisfying relationships.

For Current Providers Only

"My job is to proactively control the experiences of my clients, making their future predictable."

This statement is what I have asked more than 3,000 salespeople to write down in the past 18 months. Think about the opposite of that statement, and you will figure out what most providers are doing for even their best clients:

"My job is to be reactive and to respond to my clients' needs when they need my help, making their future questionable, but okay."

If you are the incumbent rep, the current provider, what can you do to improve your situation? How can you Wedge-proof your accounts from your competitors?

It begins with what we covered in Chapter 5 on the VISION BOX. To Wedge-proof your accounts, you first have to find out what your clients want. If I went to your very best accounts in an effort to do marketing research, and if I asked them what their service/product supplier (you) was going to do for them over the next 12, 24, or 36 months, what would they say? The probability is very high they would say that you are there for them when they need you, that you call on them regularly, and that you do a good job. I have no doubt that you have a very good relationship, which keeps you in good stead. But if one of the people I've trained to use The Wedge were to go after your account, how secure would it be? To a great degree you are very fortunate in that most of your competitors think that their service is good enough. Unfortunately for their clients, your competitors' definition of good service is mostly reactive service. Although I can't say with confidence that you or anyone else in particular is vulnerable to outside competition, I can say that many of the people I have trained in The Wedge have been remarkably successful in driving a wedge between their competition and their prospect by using their proactive services to get buyers to see they are really being underserved.

So what's the answer? If I were you, I'd have a meeting with some of the other salespeople with whom I work. I'd invite them to sit with me and do a brainstorming session. We'd play the buyer game. As buyers of your product/service, we would spend at least 30 minutes thinking of all the things we don't like about doing business with you, your firm, and your industry. We'd make a list of all the things that are difficult to understand, to predict, and therefore to control.

Let me give you an example. If I were selling health benefits to human resources (HR) directors, I'd put myself in their shoes and do the exercise. Chances are that HR directors if they really let go would have a whole list of items that they don't like because they don't understand them and therefore can't control them. Here's a short list:

How do I remain in government compliance?

How does my pricing compare with that of my competition?

What can I do when ID cards are messed up and an employee can't immediately get his or her prescription filled?

191

The list could go on, and you could do the same thing with your own industry. Just list all the items that if you were a client, you'd dislike. Once you've done that, then you can start going through the list, deciding which items you can do something about to help control your clients' experiences and make their future more predictable. Your goal in doing this is to identify areas of underservice as well as come up with the proactive services that you can use to Wedge-proof your clients, preventing your competitors from breaking them away from you.

In summary, here are three distinct things that you can do to prevent a seller from using The Wedge against you:

First, you can keep building the relationship. You will want all the relationship power you can get in order to roll your competitors when they come after your business.

Second, you can meet with your clients and do a VI-SION BOX with them. Find out exactly how they want to be served, and then put a written proactive services time line in place. Remember, your job is to proactively control your clients' experiences, making their future more predictable.

Last and by no means least, you can have a brain-storming session of the type I described. Be the client. Think about what you would want based on what you don't understand and can't control. This will be the hardest thing to do of the three things I've suggested. Many people can't get out of their own way and open up their thoughts. But if you can, you will be light-years ahead of your competition, and you will be far less vulnerable to getting fired.

CHAPTER
11

The Wedge Flight Plan: A Quick Review

At the beginning of this book, I said that selling is a lot like flying, because nothing else matters unless you land safely. In that sense, you can think of The Wedge as a flight plan. It provides a checklist of things that you can do before, during, and after each flight to make sure that you set your wheels on the runway safely, that you get paid, and that you remain ready for the next flight.

Using Red Hot Introductions, you can leverage your top clients for personal introductions to your most desirable prospects instead of just picking the lowest-hanging fruit on the tree. Then, using the Wedge precall research strategy, you can create the powerful differentiation you need to gain altitude and give your prospect a reason to buy from you. You can take your prospect through the six steps of The Wedge Sales Call, putting yourself in a position to win. As you approach the runway toward the end of your flight, you will have fended off your competition, ensuring that you touch down safely and win the business. Finally, back on the ground, you can keep your new client happy, and remain flight-ready for other missions, by using the written proactive customer services time line to make your client's future more predictable. In your debriefing, you can celebrate having done it again. You got your competition fired—without saying anything bad about them.

Before we conclude, let's review the strategy and tactics of The Wedge one last time in light of what they mean to your own sales career. As a salesperson myself, I understand that the important work you do is sometimes not fully appreciated. Salespeople make economic progress possible, and yet the sales profession is sometimes the target of unwarranted criticism based on inaccurate stereotypes. To be sure, every profession has its bad apples. The truth is that selling is an honorable way to make a living with enormous value to society. If this book helps you achieve your financial and personal goals sooner than you otherwise would have, and if it helps to increase the good that you accomplish by bringing truly proactive service to more clients, that will be my reward for having written it. So let's review.

The Strategy to Win

As we discussed, most major selling opportunities involve three parties—the seller, the buyer, and the seller's competition—a fact overlooked by traditional selling that keeps many salespeople from winning more new business.

The Wedge enables you to accomplish two things that traditional selling does not. First, it gives you a strategy for busting the relationship between your prospect and your competition. Second, it gives you a way to powerfully differentiate yourself so that your prospect will be motivated to do business with you, without your having to criticize your competition or directly promote yourself. Using The Wedge, you can get your competition fired, winning more new business with greater predictability.

Your prospects' "pain" regarding their current service is the force you will use to drive a "wedge" between them and your competitors. As mentioned in Chapter 1, about

65 to 70 percent of human motivation is pain avoidance, while only 30 to 35 percent is pleasure seeking.

Many companies today compete on price, product, and reactive service. Your greatest competitive advantage can be found in your proactive service. Proactive service consists of the day-to-day, concrete things you do that enable you to proactively control your clients' experiences and make their future more predictable. Your precall research should match your proactive service strengths against your competition's proactive service weaknesses.

There are three ways you can have a competitive advantage in services. First, you can do something unique. Second, you can do what others do, but using a better process that gets better results. Third, you can so compellingly differentiate what you do that your prospects prefer to do business with you.

You should use the ladder of abstraction to describe *how* your service is provided, using specific, concrete words that create a visual image in the mind of your prospect. Avoid generalities and abstractions.

The Tactics That Work

The Wedge Sales Call is a six-step conversation that you can use to take your prospects on a journey of self-discovery. Unlike traditional selling, it empowers you (1) to bust the relationship between your prospects and your competition and (2) to bring out your prospects' pain even though they did not at first know where they hurt because they had lowered their service expectations. Their pain had become latent rather than active.

To create rapport with your prospects in order to have an open, honest dialogue, you can match and mirror them to make them more comfortable, and you can tell a success story concerning a client like them to establish your own credibility. Next, to set the stage for the six steps, you will begin asking questions to trigger your prospects' active and latent pain.

Step 1 is to ask a PICTURE PERFECT question that gets your prospects to see the gap between their current service and the ideal service they could be receiving. Closing this painful gap is what you have to sell.

Step 2 is to TAKE AWAY the benefit you have just gotten your prospects to imagine. You will do this by suggesting that it may not be that important. If your prospects disagree, then you will know that the benefit *does* matter.

Step 3 is to use the VISION BOX to get your clients to describe in specific, concrete words exactly what they want so that you can box it for them as deliverables.

Step 4 is to REPLAY those deliverables to your prospects, confirming that you understand what they say they want.

Step 5 is to wave a WHITE FLAG and, instead of asking for the business, ask your prospects what they would like you to do. Instead of proposing something to them, you are getting them to invite you in.

Step 6 is to take your prospects through a REHEARSAL of how they will go about firing or not hiring your competition, so that you can get them to affirm to you that they will take action.

If you practice the conversational format of The Wedge Sales Call, writing PICTURE PERFECT questions and role-playing the dialogue with someone else, you should be able to start using and benefiting from The Wedge quickly. Here are the segues to remember:

PICTURE PERFECT: *"I'm curious. When you receive* [a specific service] *so that you don't have to worry about* [a specific pain], *are you comfortable with that process?"*

TAKE AWAY: *"Well, perhaps it's not that important because* [insert a reason]."

VISION BOX: *"In regard to* [area of concern], *what would you like to see happen?"*

REPLAY: *"Here's what I'm hearing you say you want.* [repeat what the prospect said.] *Have I got that right?"*

WHITE FLAG: *"So, what would you like me to do?"*

REHEARSAL: *"That's the easy part. May we talk about the hard part? . . . How will you tell your other rep that it's over?"* . . .

"Are you comfortable with everything? So it's done. Great. I'll get to work."

As you start winning more accounts using The Wedge, you can keep and grow them by making sure you create and follow a written proactive services time line to ensure that you—say it with me one last time—proactively control your clients' experience and make their future more predictable.

Changing the Way Selling Is Done

Using The Wedge, many sales professionals have been able to achieve greater personal success than before. Using The Wedge Sales Culture, numerous companies have put their profitable growth on a higher trajectory.

The Wedge benefits all three parties in the selling situation. It helps prospects by giving them a process that focuses them on their most important needs; it helps current providers by giving them an incentive to serve their clients more proactively; and, of course, it helps salespeople by giving them a powerful tool to win more clients in much less time by working smarter.

As a result, The Wedge creates healthier business relationships for everyone concerned. Buyers more likely get what they want, sellers more likely provide it, and a seller's competitors more likely try harder to please their clients.

A Final Word

So, I'm curious. When you finished this book and went out and won a major account by getting your competition fired, so that you wouldn't have to worry about falling short of your quota, how did it go? Were you comfortable with the process? Good. Well, perhaps it's not that important because traditional selling might have worked. Oh, but you're saying traditional selling pretty much limited you to prospects where you didn't have to oust a current provider? I see what you're saying.

Well, in regard to what you've learned in this book, what would you like to see happen? I see. Here's what I'm hearing you say you want. You want to keep using a proven strategy for winning top prospects away from your competitors. Have I got that right? Good.

So, what would you like me to do? You'd like me to convince you that you should stop selling and start winning? I hope that's been the easy part. May we talk about the hard part?

Suppose you waver a little at first. Let's say you revert to old habits and still manage to close enough deals with traditional selling to earn a living. May I tell you what will happen? You'll miss an opportunity to take your sales success to a whole new level. Do you really want to pass up that opportunity? Or would you rather master an approach that will enable you to win much more new business more quickly and more predictably? Yes, you would prefer that?

Are you comfortable with everything? So it's done. Great. Now go get your competition fired.

References

Berne, Eric. 1977. *Games People Play*. New York: Random House.

Brooks, Michael. 1990. *Instant Rapport*. New York: Time Warner International.

Coram, Robert. 2002. *Boyd: The Fighter Pilot Who Changed the Art of War*. New York: Little, Brown.

Hayakawa, S.I. 1989. *Language in Thought and Action*. Boston: Heinle.

Pareto, Vilfredo. 1896–1897. *Cours d'economie politique*. Lausanne: Universite de Lausanne.

Ringer, Robert J. 1976. *Winning Through Intimidation*. New York: Random House.

Slater, Robert. 1998. *Jack Welch & the G.E. Way*. New York: McGraw-Hill.

Index

Aaron, Hank, 179
Apollo XIII, 174

Berne, Eric, 149
Boyd: The Fighter Pilot Who Changed the Art of War (Coram), 180
Boy/girl theory, 102–103
Brooks, Michael, 72
Buffett, Warren, 104

Close(s):
  as goal of selling, 20
  not needed using The Wedge, 64
  REHEARSAL as the true close with The Wedge, 127, 130–131
  traditional, 23, 68, 81
Closing ratio, 36, 142, 172

CNN, 143
Competitive advantage. *See also* Strengths *vs.* weaknesses analysis
  defined, 14–15
  identifying from information, knowledge, and intelligence, 48–49
  three ways to have, 51–55
  winning difference, 42–43, 60
Consultative selling:
  defined, 23–24
  when it's adequate, 24
Contact sport, selling as a, 12, 148
Coram, Robert, 180
CRISP (continuous and rapid improvement sales process) sales meetings, 47, 149, 171, 175

Crowley, Jim. *See* Notre
    Dame's Four Horsemen
Customer retention rate, 28,
    69, 137

Dell computers, 48
Differentiation:
    based on day-to-day
        reality, 141
    branding *vs.*, 52
    lack of in insurance,
        136–137
    ladder of abstraction and,
        56–59
    one of two biggest
        problems of selling,
        20–21
    price differentiation,
        14
    proactive service as most
        powerful type of,
        129
    product differentiation,
        14
    Rules of The Wedge and,
        81–82
    strengths *vs.* weaknesses,
        80
    Wedge Flight Plan and,
        175
    Wedge Sales Culture and,
        138

EDGAR (Electronic Data
    Gathering, Analysis, and
    Retrieval System), 43
80/20 Rule, 25–26, 143–145,
    159
Eisenhower, Dwight D.,
    152

Feature benefit selling,
    23
Five money-making activities
    of salespeople, 143–145
Five-step change formula for
    a business, 155. *See also*
    Wedge Sales Culture
Four groups of a company,
    154–155. *See also* Wedge
    Sales Culture

Games People Play (Berne),
    162
Gates, Bill, 104
General Electric, 172
Gorbachev, Mikhail,
    112

Hayakawa, S.I., 56. *See also*
    Ladder of abstraction
Higginbotham & Associates,
    151
Hussein, Saddam,
    60

Industrial revolution, 22

Instant Rapport (Brooks), 71

Krantz, Gene, 175

Ladder of abstraction, 56–59, 63, 94, 108, 130, 168, 196

Laden, Elmer. *See* Notre Dame's Four Horsemen

Language in Thought and Action (Hayakawa), 56

Mantra for the salesperson, 15, 49, 129

Merriam-Webster's Collegiate Dictionary, 180

Miller, Don. *See* Notre Dame's Four Horsemen

Million Dollar Producer, 159

National Aeronautics and Space Administration (NASA), 175

Newton, Sir Isaac, 32

Notre Dame's Four Horsemen, 154

Owen, Douglas B., 149, 186

Pain:
active, 87
latent, 87
pain/pleasure motivation, 35, 195–196
potential, 87

Pareto, Vilfredo, 25, 143. *See also* 80/20 Rule

Perot, Ross, 104

PICTURE PERFECT:
five reasons won't always work, 97
key phrase, 89
step in The Wedge Sales Call, 83

Precall strategy, 39, 61, 128, 144

Proactive services time line, 54, 63, 159, 192, 198

Proactive Wedge, 93. *See also* Reactive Wedge

Prospecting. *See* Red Hot Introductions

Raiders of the Lost Ark, 68

Reactive Wedge, 92. *See also* Proactive Wedge

Reagan, Ronald, 112
Red Hot Introductions, 149,
    161–170, 194
Reid, Rusty, 151
REPLAY:
    key phrase, 115
    step in The Wedge Sales
        Call, 84
REHEARSAL:
    key phrase, 125
    step in The Wedge Sales
        Call, 84
Retention rate. *See* Customer
    retention rate
Ringer, Robert J.,
    102
Rules of The Wedge, 81–83,
    90
Ruth, Babe, 179

San Francisco State College,
    56
Securities and Exchange
    Commission, 43
SODAR (situation,
    opportunity, decision,
    action, results), 168–170
Speed, as metaphor,
    42
Strengths *vs.* weaknesses
    analysis, 50–51. *See also*
    Competitive advantage

Stuhldreher, Harry. *See*
    Notre Dame's Four
    Horsemen
Summit Global Partners,
    149–151, 186

TAKE AWAY:
    key phrase, 100
    step in The Wedge Sales
        Call, 83
Trump, Donald, 104
Two biggest problems of
    selling. *See*
    Differentiation
Two kinds of buyers and
    sellers, 187

United States Bureau of
    Labor Statistics, 180

VISION BOX:
    key phrase, 110
    step in The Wedge Sales
        Call, 84

Wal-Mart, 48
Wedge:
    based on identifying and
        using competitive
        advantage, 14–16
    based on three-party
        selling situation, 10

defined, 9
development of, 136–140
efficiency of, 60–61
ethical basis for, 12–13
expansion into The
     Wedge Sales Culture,
     148–152
necessity for pain in order
     to make it work, 35–37,
     86–89
origin of, 136–140
seven rules of, 81–83
six steps of The Wedge
     Sales Call, 83–84
Wedge Flight Plan, 194
Wedge-proofing, 54, 192
Wedge Sales Call:
based on the seven rules of
     The Wedge, 81–83
defined and outlined with
     six steps, 83–84
development of, 136–140
integration into Wedge
     Sales Culture, 148–152
key conversational phrases
     of, 131–132

part of Wedge Flight Plan,
     194
previewed, 63–64
summary of,
     196–197
used to shorten selling
     cycle, 141–142
Wedge Sales Culture:
five-step change formula,
     155
four groups of a company,
     154–155
four key roles to create
     and sustain,
     174–176
origin of name,
     151
Welch, Jack, 158
WHITE FLAG:
key phrase, 123
step in The Wedge Sales
     Call, 84
Winning with precision and
     confidence:
Gulf War and, 60
World War II and, 60

About the Author

Randy Schwantz is a leading authority and expert on the sales process. A highly successful sales professional, he is a nationally respected sales trainer, author, sales coach, consultant and public speaker. Randy is president and CEO of The Wedge Group, whose clients include Fortune 500 companies as well as small businesses. His unique sales strategy, The Wedge®, has been embraced by hundreds of companies and thousands of individual sales professionals throughout the United States and Canada. In his career, Randy has spent more than 10,000 hours talking with people who sell for a living. He and his wife, Lori, reside with their four daughters near Dallas, Texas.